# Puppy's First Christmas

## The Essential Guide for New Owners

BY SUSAN EWING

EDITORIAL
Andrew DePrisco *Editor-in-Chief*
Amy Deputato *Senior Editor*

ART
Sherise Buhagiar *Graphic Layout*
Bill Jonas *Book Design*
Brian Bengelsdorf *Cover Design*
Joanne Muzyka *Digital Art*

## Copyright © 2009

Cover photograph: long-haired Chihuahua courtesy of Gina Cioli &
Pamela Hunnicutt/BowTie, Inc.; title page photograph: Shetland
Sheepdog courtesy of Gina Cioli & Pamela Hunnicutt/BowTie, Inc.

### Kennel Club Books®

A DIVISION OF BOWTIE, INC.

40 Broad Street, Freehold, NJ 07728 USA

Library of Congress Cataloging-in-Publication Data

Ewing, Susan.
  Puppy's first christmas / by Susan Ewing.
     p. cm.
  Includes index.
  ISBN-13: 978-1-59378-649-6
  ISBN-10: 1-59378-649-2
  1. Puppies. 2. Dogs. I. Title.
  SF427.E95 2009
  636.7'0887--dc22
                                        2008002562

Printed and bound in Singapore

15 14 13 12 11 10 09     1 2 3 4 5 6 7 8 9 10

# Contents

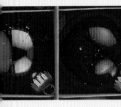

# Acknowledgments

Special thanks to Susan Chaney and the staff at *Dog Fancy* and to everyone who submitted his or her photographs. Congratulations to photo contest winners Sarah Case and Lily, Greg & Meredith Moore and Rudder, Andrea Stover and Clementine, Joyce Hayes and Elvira, Nancy Miller and Raphael and the rest of the owners of the dogs featured in this book:

Olga Lucia Acosta
Kelly Acree
Stacie Ahrens
Athena Andris
Deb Aycock
Jessica Barrett
Barbara Becker
Kelly Beneventano
Joann Blavat
Nadine Borovicka
Niki Boyd
Darlena Brill
McKenna Buck
Joyce Burgess
Carla Cameron
Tessa Coats
Krisi Deckard
Andrea DiMaio
Jan & Tom Donnell
Anife Dutcher
Scherri Edwards
Christina Fawley
Kristi Fiala
Jessica Fitch
Meriah Garnett
Sandy Garrett

Maritza Goodman
Brooke Gorman
Billie Jo Greek
Carole Greenburg
Terri Guetzlaff
Shirley Hadenfeldt
Patty Hamm
Teresa Harris
the Hess family
Marta Hinton
Shawna Hogan
Bethany Hoover
Nate & Mellissa Johnson
Tami Jones
Martha Kemp
Linda Lamon
Susan Leach
Pam Leibowitz
Lynn A. Maietta
Andrea Marra
Alisha McGraw
Jill M. Meunier
Shawn Mida
Paige Miller
Patti Mutterer
Melinda Myers

Mekayla Newsome
Deena Nunn
Bobby Pfau
Lisa Poblete
Trent J. Presser
Tracy & Jeremy Pullman
Chris Ragan
Debra Rinard
Danielle & Jerry Rocco
Michael Samano
Lisa Sapp
Sue Sell
Cassandra Silakos
Alison Silver
Teresa Snider-Boring
Vicki Sommers
Caroline Still
Andrea Stolts
Janette Thibeault
Teddi A. von Der Ahe
Kari Wade
Eugene Walker
Ruth Wilcox
Heather Wright

Additional photos: chapter openers, Tara Darling; pages 120–121, 148: Ron Kimball/www.kimballstock.com; page 65: Renee Stockdale/www.kimballstock.com

# Introduction

Before we jump headlong into the snowdrift of information on puppies, we need to take a minute to pull on our boots, so to speak. To wrap mufflers around our necks, zip up our coats and don our mittens. Okay, maybe these metaphors are a bit odd, but the point is that you need to know how I'm approaching this topic.

First, I know that there are other holidays besides Christmas, and that not everyone celebrates Christmas, but it's what I'm familiar with, what I understand. Just think of *Christmas* as my word for the entire range of festivals that occur in the days around the winter solstice. Christmas is just my winter sleigh, the vehicle I'm using to bring you packages of advice and information.

Second, I dislike calling animals "it" if I can help it. I like books that alternate masculine and feminine chapters. The trouble is, sometimes I write part of one chapter and then jump to another. I forget whether I'm writing about "him" or "her." So, in this book, for consistency's sake, the puppy is a "he."

Third, this book is not a training book, not a first-aid manual, not the definitive volume on alternative ways to feed your dog. I just want to help you get started and ease a little of the pressure of getting a puppy during the holidays. I know you're going to enjoy your dog, both as a puppy and an adult. I'm hoping this book will make raising your puppy less work and more fun.

## A PUPPY FOR CHRISTMAS

I'll get to the importance of selecting your puppy in a minute, but first I want to talk about the idea of a Christmas puppy. The consensus used to be that the holidays were absolutely the worst time to get a puppy. Many breeders would not even let their puppies go to new homes within two weeks of Christmas. Many still won't, but the thought that the holidays are a bad time to get a puppy is changing.

For over 20 years, the San Francisco SPCA has presented "Holiday Windows" from mid-November until Christmas. During this time, cats and dogs are displayed in downtown store windows for people to adopt. The dogs are walked around the area, wearing T-shirts that say, "I'm the doggie in the window." While it's true that some animals do get returned to the shelter, the number of returned pets is no greater at Christmastime than at any other time of year.

Yes, getting a puppy for Christmas means that things will be hectic and downright crazy at times, but if you understand the pitfalls and are prepared, a puppy can give the entire family a very Merry Christmas. To ease

*Lhasa Apso Charley's first Christmas-card photo.*

some of the pressure, think about what you can do before the holidays, before the puppy arrives. For instance, get those Christmas cards addressed and ready to mail in October. Halloween's a good time. You could address a card or two in between jumping up and down to answer the door when trick-or-treaters arrive.

Start your Christmas baking early and freeze it. Or, just this once, find a good bakery and have them do the baking. If your specialty is rum-soaked fruitcake or the best pumpkin bread on the planet, go ahead and make that, but let someone else worry about the rest.

As for shopping, well, if you know far enough in advance that a puppy is definitely going to be under the tree this year, get started early. Find the perfect gifts during your summer vacation. Buy stocking stuffers at holiday bazaars. Shopping for the immediate family will be easy, since what more could they possibly want than a puppy (and all of the requisite puppy accessories)?

## FINDING THE PERFECT MATCH

No matter what time of year you get a puppy, do your homework. Do you want a small dog, a medium-size dog or a giant dog? Long hair or short? Active or a couch potato? Don't just buy the first cute puppy you see. All puppies are adorable, but you have to consider what your puppy will be like as an adult. Some pups grow up

*Pug Cubbie is a true gift to his family.*

to weigh 150 pounds or more, while others stay under 5 pounds. Of course, there is a range of sizes in between. What will fit your family and lifestyle best?

If you have a studio apartment, a giant breed like the Great Dane may not be the wisest choice. The other extreme is the toy dog, which, generally speaking, is not a good idea for a family with small children. Toy dogs are fragile and can get hurt, and toddlers

*Chihuahua Marla packs lots of love into a small package.*

can't always judge how roughly they may be playing with a dog. On the other hand, a bouncy 70-pound puppy can easily knock over small children or scratch them with his nails.

Consider how much grooming you're willing to do. Dogs with long hair will need more brushing and trimming than dogs with shorter coats. Remember, though, that just because a dog is short-coated doesn't mean that he won't shed. Short-haired dogs mean lots of short hairs that can work their way into upholstery and carpeting. Some dogs, like Poodles and Bichons Frises, don't shed, but they need regular grooming every four to six weeks, or their hair will become tangled and matted. Add the cost of grooming sessions to your budget if you choose one of these dogs.

If you're considering a purebred, think about what the dog was bred for, its requirements and its temperament. The best way to know just what a specific breed will be like is to talk to reputable breeders. Go to the American Kennel Club's Web site, www.akc.org, where you can find links to the Web sites of each breed's national club. Club sites usually include breeder contact information, so you can search for breeders in your area. You can also talk to people who own the breed.

If you plan to make your selection at the local animal shelter, there may be many mixed breeds waiting for adoption. Try to determine what went into the mix. What does

**RESCUE PUP**

Consider adopting from a local rescue organization. There are breed-specific rescues as well as groups that take in all breeds and mixed breeds. Dogs are usually housed in foster homes instead of in a shelter facility.

*How about some Christmas chocolate (Labs, that is) under the tree?*

the dog look like? Does he resemble a German Shepherd, a Scottish Terrier, something in between or something totally different? It's not always easy to determine a mixed-breed dog's parentage, but knowing what's in the mix, if possible, will help you know a bit about what it will be like to live with that particular dog.

You can always just pick the dog that seems to have picked you! There are worse ways to get a dog, and if it turns out that he digs a bit or has a stubborn streak, well, nobody's perfect. All dogs, pure-bred and mixed alike, can have behavior quirks that you will have to deal with, and no matter how you pick your puppy or where you get him from, it is your responsibility to work through any problems that arise. This is your new family member, and every puppy deserves full commitment from his owners.

## A GIFT FOR THE WHOLE FAMILY
Also think about who's going to do what. Just because your child wants a puppy and you say that it's "hers" doesn't mean that your child can, or will, or should

do all of the work involved in having a puppy. Ultimately, the responsibility has to lie with an adult. That doesn't mean that your children shouldn't help. It does mean that chores have to be age appropriate and that if a child forgets to perform a chore, like giving the dog fresh water or food, then you need to do it.

So, how old are your children? Even a three-year-old can learn to be gentle and help "groom" a puppy by running a soft cloth or baby brush over the dog. When you take the dog out, let your five-year old hold the leash with you and learn how to walk the

*You know Dasher and Dancer and Prancer and... Lucas?*

## SUPERSTITIONS

We might all be happy to get a dog at Christmas, but in the past, dogs weren't so welcome at this time of year. In Scotland, stray dogs were portents of evil, so they were chased away. In the not-so-good-old-days, it was believed that dogs that howled on Christmas Eve were fated to go mad before the end of the year.

# ALL I WANT FOR CHRISTMAS...

Another advantage to getting a puppy during the holidays is that making your Christmas list will be easy. You won't have much to return or exchange this year if you ask friends and relatives for puppy-related gifts. Of course, some of these items you will need to have on hand before puppy's arrival, but here are some ideas to get you started:

- ✔ A sturdy crate for use in the home and possibly a second crate for travel
- ✔ Collar and leash
- ✔ Food and water dishes
- ✔ Dog bed
- ✔ Toys
- ✔ Brushes and combs
- ✔ Doggie coat or sweater
- ✔ Pet-supply store gift certificate
- ✔ Gift certificates toward obedience lessons, grooming sessions, boarding or dog-sitting
- ✔ Bait bag
- ✔ Training books
- ✔ Breed books (if applicable)
- ✔ Identification tags

puppy. A seven-year old can fill a water bowl or meas-
ure out dog food, and older children can help with
training.

Before the puppy comes home, make out a basic
chart for chores, including the time for each particular
chore and whose responsibility it is, and post it on the
refrigerator. There may be adjustments once there's
actually a dog to care for, but the chart will give you
a starting point and will be a good reminder to family
members as to who needs to do what and when it
needs to happen. That way, there won't be any argu-
ments about who was supposed to fill the water bowl.

*Happy "howl"idays from these caroling Plott pups.*

# GETTING TO KNOW PUREBREDS

The American Kennel Club divides its recognized breeds into seven groups, Working, Sporting, Hound, Terrier, Toy, Non-sporting and Herding, based on the breeds' original functions and abilities. While each breed is unique, breeds that are grouped together do share some general characteristics, and looking at the breed groups can be a good place to start when researching which purebred is the best match for your family.

**Working Group:** Working dogs are generally large. They may be intimidating. Many are very good with children, but they may also be stubborn and harder to train.

**Sporting Group:** Sporting breeds frequently need lots of exercise. They were bred to help hunters locate quarry and may be more inclined to follow a trail than to want to play. This is a generalization, of course, because Labrador Retrievers and Golden Retrievers, two of the best family breeds around, love nothing more than playing fetch (unless it's diving into the water).

**Hound Group:** There are two types of hounds: those that hunt by sight (sighthounds) and those that use their noses to follow a trail (scenthounds). Hounds, as a group, are independent and can be stubborn. Both sighthounds and scenthounds can be very focused on what they are chasing. You need a securely fenced yard with these dogs.

**Terrier Group:** Terriers were bred to dig, so if you prize your flowerbed or want a perfect lawn, you might not want a terrier. Terriers are also tough little dogs who won't back down in a fight. Their size makes them appealing, as many terriers are smaller dogs, but they still need to get exercise.

**Toy Group:** Toy breeds are small, sometimes fragile, dogs who were bred as companions. Toys can be charming, but they may not be the best choice for families with young children, who may be too rough for such a small dog. If you're after a companion to cuddle with, though, there's nothing better than a toy breed.

**Non-sporting Group:** The Non-sporting Group is different from the other groups in that the breeds are quite varied. From the energetic Dalmatian to the clownish French Bulldog to the affectionate Bichon Frise, this group includes quite a few breeds with friendly, outgoing personalities that make good family dogs.

**Herding Group:** Herding dogs generally make loyal family pets and many are very willing and talented when it comes to playing games. The herding instinct means that many herding dogs like to keep the entire family together in one place, and that can include "rounding up" the children by chasing and nipping at them. This is neither aggressive behavior nor biting, but part of the herding routine and something that needs to be considered.

# Oh, Bring Us Some Figgy Pudding

## BOWL BASICS

You've got your puppy—now what? One of the very basic elements of care is supplying your dog with good food and fresh water. Let's first discuss what you're going to use to hold that food and water. You've got some choices as to exactly what kind of dishes to use. Unbreakable bowls top my list, but there are some very cute ceramic dog dishes on the market, and many of them have the advantage of being heavy and therefore hard to tip over. Just make sure that if your choice is ceramic, it is coated with a lead-free glaze.

Plastic is a popular choice, but it can be hard to get plastic bowls really clean, especially if sharp little puppy teeth have scratched or chewed on them. Also, if your puppy has a short, flat face, rubbing on the plastic can lead to a case of acne. If you decide on plastic, pop those dishes in the dishwasher to make sure they get thoroughly clean.

Stainless steel is a terrific choice. It is easy to wash and unbreakable, and some stainless bowls are weighted or have rubber on the bottom to prevent tipping and to keep them in place.

*Cookies, milk and Lola, waiting for Santa's arrival.*

No matter what kind of food you choose for your dog, serve it in a clean bowl, and no matter what kind of bowl you choose, wash the bowl after every meal! Sure, that bowl looks clean—your puppy has licked up every morsel of food! But that doesn't mean that the bowl *is* clean. You wouldn't put your dinner plate back in the cupboard just because you'd licked it clean.

You also need a bowl for water, and this bowl should be kept full of fresh clean water. Even small dogs will drink about a quart of water a day, and all dogs will drink more in warmer weather. Many puppies think there's nothing better than paddling in their water dishes, so be sure to refill the bowl as needed.

## DIET DOS AND DON'TS

Buying the right bowls is only a small part of the battle. In the hustle and bustle of preparing for the holidays and the addition of a puppy to the family, remember to add dog food to your grocery list. Most breeders will send home a two- or three-day supply of whatever food your puppy is used to eating. If you get your puppy from a shelter, ask what the pup's being fed and buy some of that food. In spite of the fact that puppies will try to eat anything and everything, they can have sensitive stomachs. If you introduce a new diet along with the stress of a new home, you're asking for digestive trouble.

Stick to whatever your puppy is used to for at least a week. Then, if you want to change brands, make the change gradual. Whatever your puppy's portion, make it two-thirds of his old food and one-third of the new for a day. Then, the next day, make it half and half. On the third day, give one-third of the old with two-thirds of the new, and by day four, feed only the new food.

Dog meals aren't as complex as people meals. If you choose to feed a commercial dog food, it's one bowl, one food, and gone in one instant. Still, a walk down the pet-food aisle at the grocery or pet-supply store shows you that there are plenty of choices.

Basically, you can feed dry, canned or semi-moist dog food. Dry food is the most economical and keeps the longest. It gives your puppy something to chew, although many dogs seem to simply inhale their food and don't use

*Surprise! It's Dogue de Bordeaux
pup Aneli under the tree.*

their teeth much at all. If you decide to free-feed your puppy—that is, leave food out all the time—dry food is the way to go. If you do decide on dry food, remember that the size of the kibble does make a difference. Smaller dogs need a smaller, denser piece of kibble to get all the nutrients they need. If you have a small-breed puppy, choose a food with a small kibble.

Canned food would probably be your puppy's choice if he had a vote. Canned food is generally meat-based and, to a dog, smells terrific. Canned food is more expensive than dry, and any unused portions have to be refrigerated once the can is open. Included in the canned-food category are the pouches of food that generally look like slices of meat in gravy.

Semi-moist foods are frequently shaped to look like ground meat, beef patties or chops. They don't need refrigeration and may cost the same as, or more than, canned foods. Semi-moist foods generally have more flour, sugar and coloring than either dry or canned foods, none of which your dog needs.

No matter what type of food you choose, go with premium brands. You may have to experiment with the kind your dog likes best, as some foods are too rich for some dogs. Also, your dog may be allergic to a certain ingredient, in which case you would have to try foods that do not contain that ingredient.

Study the labels when you choose your food. All dog-food labels should include a statement from AAFCO,

## TINY TUMMIES

While it's okay to toss puppy a safe tidbit now and then, remember that small puppies have small and sensitive stomachs. It won't take much to be too much of a good thing!

which stands for American Association of Feed Control Officials, the governing body for all animal feeds. They set the guidelines for pet-food manufacturers. For instance, meat by-products may not include hair, horns, teeth, hooves, feathers or manure. Another AAFCO requirement is that ingredients must be listed in order of their percentage in the food, from the most to the least, including preservatives.

When you're reading the label, pay particular attention to the first five ingredients. Somewhere in those first five, and preferably in first place, should be

*Merry Christmas from Samson Claus!*

*Six-month-old Jack waits patiently for his presents.*

a meat protein. This is frequently beef, chicken, turkey or lamb. Some foods may list fish or something a bit more exotic, like venison, as a protein. Meat or chicken by-products may be listed in the top five as well. "By-products" translates into organ meat, including stomachs and intestines, which sounds icky but in fact can contain lots of vitamins and minerals. Next, there will probably be a grain filler. Even canned foods will include a filler. The grain adds bulk to the food, but there should be more meat than filler. The most common grains are corn, wheat, rice and soy. Corn is the cheapest, so it's the grain you're most likely to see. If your dog shows an allergic reaction, which is commonly manifested in his biting or chewing at his paws, it's likely that he's allergic to the grain filler. Rice causes fewer reactions, so it's becoming a very popular filler. Vitamins and minerals will be next on the label, and then preservatives. Preservatives are more likely in dry and semi-moist foods than in canned foods.

Other dietary choices include home cooked and raw food, the latter frequently called the BARF diet. That stands for Bones and Raw Foods or Biologically Appropriate Raw Foods. With either of these choices, you need to know how to make sure that your dog gets a balanced diet. A balanced raw diet is not just meaty bones, and a balanced home-cooked meal is not just ground meat and rice. Raw diets include organ meats and vegetables as well as vitamin supplements. Home-cooked meals also need the right balance between protein, carbohydrates, vitamins and minerals. If you decide you want to follow one of these menus, there are several books on the market that can teach you what you need to know.

Besides basic meals, your puppy will get treats. Treats are wonderful aids to training, and sometimes it's just fun to give your dog a treat for no reason at all. Treats can be dog biscuits, but they also can be things like the crust from your pizza or a piece of cheese as you're making lunch. Whatever treats you give your puppy, remember that treats count toward your puppy's overall calorie count. Limit treats to 10 percent of your puppy's daily food intake.

Taking it easy with the treats can be hard to do, but it is important, especially during the holidays, when there tends to be more food around for both humans and dogs. If you're having a party, this may be the time to crate your puppy. Oh, sure, let everyone see him when guests first arrive. It's good socialization, and everyone will want to ooh and aah over the latest member of the family. Then say goodnight and crate your puppy. This makes it easier for everyone to resist the temptation to share a canapé with the canine. You don't want the puppy to get stuffed or to have an upset tummy

## SPECIAL TREATS

Visit a local pet boutique or dog bakery to find special pet-safe holiday goodies for Fido. Just-for-dogs cookies, cupcakes and other baked snacks are adorable and much better for puppy's tummy than human hors d'oeuvres.

*Those cookies are for Santa Claus, not Santa Paws.*

from munching on goodies that are too rich for his little stomach.

Some of the holiday foods that may be available not only are fattening but also can make a dog seriously ill or even be fatal. You'll need to keep these foods well away from your puppy and let your guests know which tidbits are a no-no. Once your dog is older, you can teach him to "leave" items dropped on the floor; also, as he grows, his body can absorb more of problem foods before they become a problem. For a small puppy, just a little bit of a dangerous food can cause severe illness. An older dog might not be so curious, either, although it's been my experience that dogs are always curious if something appears to be edible.

The holidays frequently mean lots of activity in the kitchen. Fruitcakes, stollen, cookies, cakes, breads. Many of these foods contain raisins, nuts, eggs and yeast. At my house, Christmas also means chocolate. When it's time to make dinner, there may be onions. All of these products are on the "forget it" list for your puppy (and adult dog).

If you drop a raisin while making the family fruitcake and your puppy eats it, don't panic. If, however, your puppy eats a quantity of raisins, it's time for that trip to the vet. Raisins can cause kidney failure, so don't delay in getting your puppy medical attention. Grapes have the same effect. Your puppy may vomit, have diarrhea, be excessively thirsty or have abdominal pains.

Most nuts are dangerous but will not be a problem if your puppy eats just a few. The exception is macadamia nuts, which are particularly dangerous. If your puppy consumes more than one or two, his hindquarters may become paralyzed. Other symptoms include mild fever and vomiting. Depending on how many nuts your puppy eats, and what size he is, paralysis will set in within 12 to

24 hours. Fortunately, the paralysis is temporary, and your puppy should fully recover within three days.

A greater danger is that the paralysis will be misdiagnosed for something more serious. Macadamia nuts are not the only nuts that are harmful to dogs, so keep all types of nuts away from your puppy. Who wants to share something that good, anyway?

Another goody on the "do not share" list is chocolate. Keep the bon bons for yourself, and make sure your puppy doesn't get into the baking chocolate. The theobromine in chocolate can be fatal, and the darker the chocolate, the greater the danger. If your puppy steals an M & M, don't panic, but if he eats a square of baker's chocolate, get to the vet's office immediately.

I remember a verse from the song "Skip to My Lou" that went, "Chicken in the bread pan, pecking out dough." It may not have hurt the chickens, but yeast dough can hurt your puppy. On the rare occasions when I've made yeast dough, I have sometimes opened the oven door and set the bowl there for the dough to rise. That is obviously not a good choice if there's a dog in the house. The bowl would be very accessible, and yeast dough can cause a drunken appearance and cardiac arrest.

Growing up, common wisdom had it that a raw egg a week was good for a dog's coat. I don't know whether it helped the coat, but it turns out that raw egg whites contain avidin, a protein that makes it impossible for a dog to use the B vitamin biotin. So no raw eggs for Angel. Cooked eggs are fine, so if you want to share your scrambled eggs with your puppy now and then, go right ahead.

Do not, however, let the puppy wash down the eggs with coffee or tea. Both of these beverages contain caffeine and theobromine, and neither of these things is good for dogs.

Onions are another edible hazard, and while it's hard to imagine a dog eating a huge quantity of onions, puppies do seem to want to eat everything they find. Onions can cause hemolytic anemia. Symptoms include pale mucous membranes, lack of appetite and lethargy. Your puppy may feel cold or may have a fever or a fast heart rate. If the onions have disappeared, warm up the car and head for the vet's office. A blood transfusion or a shot of vitamin B-12 will help.

*"Santa, is that you?" wonders Lola.*

Xylitol is an artificial sweetener that used to be used mostly in sugarless gums, but it's now showing up as a substitute for sugar in baking. Xylitol consumption in dogs can result in depression, loss of coordination and seizures.

Christmas means friends dropping in, and that can mean a glass of Christmas cheer. Remember that alcohol is for humans only. Don't let your puppy drink any alcoholic beverage. A drunken dog isn't funny, and even a small amount of liquor can cause alcohol poisoning, which, in turn, can kill your dog. Further, although this isn't a food product, the nicotine in tobacco products can be deadly. Keep all cigars, cigarettes, snuff and chewing tobacco out of reach of your puppy.

# Not-So-Silent Nights

## 3

## ALL IS CALM

It's a nice sentiment, but it's not a likely occurrence during the holidays. Even if you try to limit activities and company, that in itself can be a real challenge. So, have the grandparents for their annual visit, but maybe you shouldn't host the school Christmas party this year. In spite of your best efforts, there will be all the hustle and bustle of shopping and wrapping presents as well as decorating the house, picking just the right tree, stringing the lights, baking tray after tray of cookies, cooking large meals and having friends and relatives over to visit. After Christmas, there will still be friends and relatives in and out and a frenzy of cleaning for the New Year's Eve party. Kids will be out of school and underfoot. Fun, but not calm.

Adding a puppy is going to add to the frenzy! That's not necessarily bad, but you need to understand that, like a baby, that puppy is going to need attention and care as a priority, no matter what else is going on. Also like a baby, that puppy will need some calm times. Puppies need quiet corners for naps. For lots of naps. That's one of the reasons you'll need a crate, which will be explained

*Gus is dreaming of reindeer games.*

in more detail in the chapter on house-training. The crate is the place for naps and for keeping the puppy safe and out of harm's way.

Even though someone will always be supervising the puppy when he's not crated, puppies are amazingly fast and can get into trouble quickly. For this reason, you'll need to puppy-proof your home. Puppies can't open closed cupboard doors, but they can nudge open any doors that are ajar. Keep doors shut tight so your puppy doesn't accidentally get into cleaning products or eat an entire box of cereal. Cover or tape down electrical cords or run them through a length of PVC pipe. Invest in a baby gate or two to keep your puppy contained in one room or to keep him out of forbidden rooms.

## SETTLED IN FOR A LONG WINTER'S NIGHT

With a puppy in the house, your nights may not be silent, especially the first couple of nights. Your puppy may whine and cry. His mother is gone, his brothers and sisters are gone, he's in a strange house with strange people, he's lonely and he's going to tell the world. If possible, let him sleep in someone's bedroom at night. He doesn't have to share anyone's bed, but just being in a room with someone will help him feel less lonely. If he won't tear it to shreds, give him a stuffed toy to cuddle up next to. That will remind him of his littermates.

Another option is a SnugglePuppie. This is a stuffed toy with a heating unit and a "heartbeat" that will remind your puppy of his mother's heartbeat (www.snuggleme.com). Your puppy may still fuss a bit, but just harden your heart and eventually he'll drift off to sleep. My male, Griffin, tore my heart out during his first two weeks at home. For 15 to 20 minutes each night, he would cry loudly and pathetically, and then he'd fall asleep. It was not a pleasant sound, but we lived through it and so will you.

It may help if your puppy is tired when you retire for the night, so plan a little playtime just before bedtime. Give your puppy something to eat as well. It doesn't have to be much, but a full stomach will help your puppy drift off into dreamland. Play first and then feed. Making sure

*Wake up, Clementine. It's Christmas morning!*

the puppy is warm and in a draft-free area will also help get the puppy drowsy. Just writing this is making me yawn.

## OVER THE RIVER AND THROUGH THE WOODS

Holidays frequently mean travel, and that may mean that your puppy is traveling as well. If your puppy is under six months old, he probably doesn't have all of his shots, and boarding kennels won't generally board a dog that has not had all of the required vaccinations. That limits your choices to leaving the puppy with a pet sitter or taking the puppy with you.

If you choose to take the puppy along, take his health and vaccination records with you. If your puppy has been microchipped, that's great. If your puppy gets lost while you're traveling, a chip (which contains your contact information) can help reunite him with you if he is found. But even with a microchip, it's a good idea to have ID tags on your dog's collar. If you're going to be staying at one destination for a while, have a second tag made with that information. If you lose your puppy in Kentucky, it's not going to help if the phone number on the tag is your phone in Pennsylvania. Of course, if you have a cell phone, you can just use that number. Don't forget your puppy's leash for rest stops and walks.

Take enough of your puppy's food to last the entire vaca-

## TRAVEL PREP

Before attempting a long car trip with pup, accustom him to the car by taking a few short trips around town or even just around the block. Many dogs love to go for rides in the car, but a little preparation never hurts.

tion. Don't assume that you'll be able to buy your brand at your destination. Take water from home as well to help prevent tummy upsets. If you're going to be gone more than a couple of days, gradually introduce him to the local water by combining it with the water you brought from home so that your dog can get used to the different water. If your puppy is on any kind of medication, take enough for the entire trip.

Pack a small first aid kit for the car (see Chapter 11) as well as extra towels for bedding, for wiping off mud or for drying your puppy if he gets wet. Carry a roll or two of paper towels also for quick clean-ups.

If you'll be staying with friends or relatives, make sure you ask first before you show up on their doorstep with a puppy. If you'll be staying at motels,

*Stylish holiday traveler Cocoa is*
*packed and ready to go.*

make sure they allow pets. AAA has a good book called *Traveling With Your Pet* that lists over 12,000 motels, hotels and inns that accept pets. Always call ahead to confirm that your puppy is welcome, though, because policies can change.

A tip for staying at motels is to carry a sheet or two to cover the beds and protect them from dirty paws or dog hair. The management won't appreciate a bedspread covered with dog hair or mud. If your car is stuffed to the roof and you don't want to carry the extra sheets, ask housekeeping for some.

Never leave your puppy alone in a room uncrated. If you do leave him alone in his crate, turn on the television

*Listening for sleigh bells keeps six-month-old Rhodesian Ridgeback Ale wide awake on Christmas Eve.*

*Seven-month-old Finnigan is
ready to show off his holiday style.*

to keep him company. The television will also mask noises that might start your puppy barking.

I tend to think of the holidays as a time of ice and snow, but maybe you're heading for someplace a bit warmer. Regardless of the temperature, remember to never leave your puppy in a closed car. Sun beating in the windows can raise the temperature in the car to over 100 degrees very quickly. Dogs rely on panting to get cool, and that's not a very efficient system. Your dog could easily die from overheating; leaving the windows partially open is dangerous, too.

**WAKE-UP CALL**

Don't be annoyed with your pup when he whines or barks to go outside in the middle of the night. It's an adjustment period for both of you, but stick it out and soon you'll both be sleeping through the night.

*In the role of Rudolph is eight-month-old Hercules, the red-nosed Dogue de Bordeaux.*

If you're staying where it's cold and icy, remember that cold can also be deadly. A car can get very cold, and that cold can threaten your puppy's life. Small dogs lose body heat more quickly than large dogs do, so a chill that might not bother an adult may be too much for your puppy to handle.

If it will be easier to leave your wonderful puppy behind, you'll need a pet sitter. Pet sitters come to your home at scheduled times to feed, walk and play with your dog. You may need extra visits for a puppy, or you may want to get a sitter who will spend the night. Pet sitters cost more than kennels, but they may also water plants and bring in your mail as well as care for your dog. If you are wary about someone else being in your home or want to save the expense, puppy sitting could be a job for a willing friend or relative.

If your puppy is over six months old, you can board him at a kennel. Think of a kennel as camp for your dog. He will have his own private run, and there may be scheduled play times as well. Fees will vary, and all kennels have different rules about what you can bring. Some kennels will charge extra for giving medicines or feeding different foods. Ask about check-in and check-out times. Ask how the kennel staff handles emergencies. If possible, visit the kennel before you board your dog. Kennels should be clean, and fences should all be in good repair, with no sharp edges or broken pieces. All kennel areas should be well maintained, and the staff should be knowledgeable and caring.

It's hard to leave a dog at a kennel when he is looking pathetic and you can almost hear him saying, "Don't leave me," but again, harden your heart. Young dogs especially adjust very quickly to being boarded. A kennel may not be home, but your puppy will be safe and will greet you with lots of kisses when you pick him up after your trip.

*Yorkie Sugar sleeps better when she*
*has a friend to cuddle with.*

## CHRISTMAS BOOKS

I love Christmas, dogs and books, so when I find a book about a dog at Christmas, I'm as happy as a dog with a chew toy. Here's a partial list. Some have been made into television specials, so if you can't find the book, check your TV listings.

• *How the Grinch Stole Christmas* by Dr. Seuss. Max the dog might not be the main character, but I love him.

• *Olive, the Other Reindeer* by Vivian Walsh. A small dog named Olive misunderstands the song lyrics "all of the other reindeer," and thinks she's supposed to be at the North Pole helping Santa.

• *The Night Before Christmas* by Clement Clarke Moore, illustrated by Tasha Tudor. This version of the classic has a Corgi on hand to greet St. Nick and help him distribute the presents.

• *Carl's Christmas* by Sandra Day. The wonderful Rottweiler Carl takes the baby shopping and caroling before they all fall asleep before the fire.

• *MacDuff's New Friend* by Rosemary Wells, illustrated by Susan Jeffers. The intrepid Westie knows there's an intruder in the shed. What a surprise for the entire family when that intruder turns out to be Santa Claus.

• *The Shepherd, the Angel and Walter the Christmas Miracle Dog* by Dave Barry. Dave Barry is always good for a smile, but this story is also touchingly sweet.

• *Christmas Dog* by Joy Cowley, illustrated by Astrid Matijasevic. The puppy the parents choose is young, is noisy, is not house-trained, chews things and will be a lot of work . . . just like the children. But it will also be a lot of fun, just like the children.

• *Henry and Mudge and a Very Merry Christmas* by Cynthia Rylant, illustrated by Sucie Stevenson. This book is about a boy and his Mastiff getting ready for Christmas. They bake cookies, see relatives, go caroling and give gifts. In the end, Henry knows what's really important. "Merry Christmas, Mudge," Henry said. "You're still the best present of all."

• *Clifford's Christmas* by Norman Bridwell. The big red dog is at it again, and his family knows he's the best. "Clifford is a wonderful dog. He makes every day Christmas Day."

• *Old Dog Cora and the Christmas Tree* by Consie Powell. An old Newfoundland won't break with tradition when it comes time to bring home the Christmas tree.

# Toyland

## 4

This is where spending money on your puppy becomes fun. Puppies love toys, and Christmas is your chance to present your pup with a great big stocking full of all types of toys. Some stores sell already-stuffed stockings for dogs, and these typically include a couple of toys, a rawhide or real bone and doggy treats. If you opt for this type of stocking, make sure you buy one that's size appropriate and that you approve of the toys and treats.

If someone in your family enjoys craft projects, your puppy can have a homemade stocking with his name on it. Or you can buy a stocking specially made for a dog. Variety stores and pet-supply shops will have these in stock. You may even find one with your specific breed on it. However you decide to go, remember that, given the chance, your puppy will consider the stocking a toy in itself. If you want to use the stocking year after year, keep it away from sharp puppy teeth this year.

Now for the stocking stuffers. First, remember the size of your puppy. A tennis ball in the toe of the stocking is a great idea for large-breed puppies, but it will just frustrate a Toy Poodle or Chihuahua-size puppy. Find a smaller, hard rubber ball for those canines. You can also

*Four-and-a-half-month-old Norwich Terrier Louie relaxes with Mr. Elf.*

use cat toys for very small puppies. These toys are scaled down and can provide just as much fun as a dog toy. One cautionary note: many cat toys are stuffed with catnip, and that won't hurt your dog, but if your puppy's sharp teeth rip the toy open, you're going to have a bunch of loose catnip to clean up.

Next on my list would be a hard rubber toy that has a hole for stuffing full of treats. These make great dog pacifiers for those times when your puppy needs to be left alone in his crate or pen. Choose a size-appropriate hard nylon bone as well for serious chew time.

Add some biscuits to the stocking, or maybe a small bag of soft treats that will come in handy during training sessions. Soft treats may have a lot of added sugar and preservatives, so limit the amount. Your pet-supply store will have all kinds of biscuits and chewies, and they may even be in Christmas colors and shapes. Ask the clerk for suggestions that will fit with your puppy's size.

Rawhide bones or chips should be given sparingly, and you should supervise your puppy with rawhide. Some dogs chew carefully, but others gulp large chunks that can make a gooey mess in the stomach or intestines and lead to throwing up or an impacted bowel that needs surgery. Some breeds, like Bulldogs, should never have rawhide. (Bulldogs tend to unravel bones and swallow as they go, never biting off a chunk.) Check out your pet-supply store for pressed rawhide bones, which are safer, as they are made out of pieces of shredded rawhide and thus pose less risk of blockage if swallowed.

Dogs love cow hooves, but they can be too hard for tiny puppy jaws to tackle and, to put it politely, they smell. Pigs' ears can stain carpeting; for that matter, any smoked bone may stain fabric, and, if you live where there are cold winters, you can't put a puppy outdoors to chew a bone.

Most dogs love squeaky latex toys, but many consider the squeaker to be the best part. They will chew around it and try to dislodge the squeaker, which is a hard plastic piece that poses danger if swallowed, so supervise your pup with these types of toys. If the toy becomes ripped or punctured, take the toy away from the

*Rammu is dreaming of all the puppy*
*toys he'll soon find under the tree.*

*Shih Tzu Sa Dee celebrates by tearing into her gifts.*

dog. If your puppy chews the squeaky part out, take it away from him and throw it away.

Tug toys can be fun, but be cautious when using them with puppies. A puppy's tiny teeth are not permanent, and you could loosen them or pull them out by playing tug with your pup. Also, the puppy himself is still growing, without the strength he might need to play without harming himself.

Some dog toys are animated, making noises or erratic movements, and these will seem like prey for your puppy. He'll have lots of fun trying to catch and "kill" these types of toys, and you'll have fun watching him in action.

My favorite stocking topper is a stuffed toy, and most dogs adore them. Many dogs also like to see just how fast they can destroy a stuffed toy so, again, supervise play.

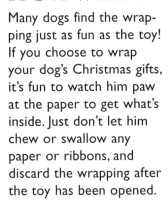

## IT'S A WRAP!

Many dogs find the wrapping just as fun as the toy! If you choose to wrap your dog's Christmas gifts, it's fun to watch him paw at the paper to get what's inside. Just don't let him chew or swallow any paper or ribbons, and discard the wrapping after the toy has been opened.

Your puppy may just want to cuddle with the toy or carry it around in his mouth, with only gentle chewing. Or your puppy may be like my Corgis, whose goal is to reach the plastic squeaky in the center of the toy as fast as possible. This doesn't stop me from giving them stuffed toys, but I buy the cheapest toys I can find, and I offer them the toys only when I can spend a half hour or so watching them play.

Once the toy is ripped open, I remove the squeaker and the poly-fiber filling so that the dogs won't choke on it. Be prepared for very slimy hands, as your puppy will have thoroughly wet the toy as he chews it open. Some dogs are happy to carry around the plush outer shell, and some will completely lose interest once the toy no longer squeaks.

I have tried toys that made other types of noises besides squeaks, but with mixed results. The toys I chose were a combination of tough plastic and plush, and instead of squeaking, a voice said something like, "Hey dog breath, quit chewing on me." This seemed cute until

*"Santa, what do you have in here for me?"*

*Faithful guardian of the gifts.*

my girl started biting it. Then it was, "Hey dog breath, quit chewing on me," nonstop. Fortunately, she "killed" the toy in less than 15 minutes. With my male, every time he bit it and heard the voice, he'd stop chewing as though someone had scolded him. So now I'm back to toys that squeak.

All of these toys make great stocking stuffers, but you can also improvise and give your dog inexpensive playthings. Just remember to supervise. What works well with one dog may be a disaster with another. Here's an example: when my male was a puppy, he discovered a paper bag full of empty soda cans in the kitchen. He tipped the bag over and loved all the shiny,

## THAT'S NOT A TOY!

Since puppies will chew and enjoy just about anything, you might be tempted to give your puppy an old shoe or a sock tied in a knot. The problem with that idea is that dogs don't discriminate between "old and worthless" and "new and expensive." They will easily make the transition from old shoes to your best pair, and it will be very hard, if not impossible, to explain the difference. So don't start. The same goes for old clothing of any kind. Invest in some proper dog toys. It will be much less expensive in the long run.

noisy toys that spilled all over the floor. He liked chasing a rolling can and batting it around. Everything was fine until he discovered he could also bite the soft aluminum. A can with several bites in it was no longer a smooth, safe toy but had sharp edges that could harm a puppy, so that play session was over.

My female, Rhiannon, doesn't care for something that makes that kind of racket, so she's never played with cans. She does enjoy the occasional cardboard tube from a roll of paper towels or toilet paper. Another idea is to put a paper grocery bag on the floor and let your puppy go in and out or chew it up. Never let your puppy play with plastic bags, though, as he

*"What do I play with first?" wonders Maltese pup Snowball.*

# THE CHRISTMAS ELEPHANT

It was Christmastime and we had gotten out our decorations, including our traditional Christmas elephant. Don't ask for a connection between Christmas and an elephant. Someone, sometime, had given us a small red elephant, wearing a thin green ribbon around its neck. I don't know whether it was intended as a Christmas decoration or not, but since it was red and green, we always put it out at Christmas.

One evening, we left the dogs alone while we attended a concert. When we returned home, we opened the door and were greeted by three happy dogs. Beyond them, I could see through to the living room. Our ice-blue carpeting was covered with reddish smears. Great swirls of color. Blood. I was terrified that one of the dogs was injured and, on another level, was trying to think how on earth we'd ever get all those bloodstains out of the carpet.

All of the dogs seemed fine. None was bleeding, and I couldn't find any cuts, so we went into the living room for a closer look. What I had thought was blood was something resembling sawdust. Next to a chair were the limp remains of our Christmas elephant.

When things get destroyed in a household full of dogs, it's generally the puppy who's at fault. I suspected the puppy had "killed" the elephant, but it could have been an older dog because all my Corgis have a keen interest in disemboweling stuffed toys. Anyway, I'll never know because the dogs aren't telling.

could accidentally suffocate or chew off and swallow pieces that will block his intestines.

Plastic milk or juice bottles can amuse a puppy. Put a handful of uncooked macaroni or rice inside a plastic bottle to make the toy rattle. (Avoid pennies or pebbles, as neither is a good thing for a puppy to swallow if the bottle gets punctured or pops open.)

A piece of clothesline knotted in several places can make a good toy for carrying around or for chewing. Replace when it gets dirty or very frayed.

If you live on or near a farm, the rubber inserts on automatic milking machines make great toys. They are durable and safe and can be washed in the dishwasher.

Let your imagination be your guide when it comes to toys. Just keep safety in mind at all times.

*Boston Terrier pup Coco loves her new Santa toy.*

Just because you have a puppy doesn't mean you can't "deck the halls." Decorating is a huge part of the holiday season, and you can still have your tree and your garlands, your candles and your plants. You just need to use a bit of caution and remember that puppies are like two-year-olds. They are fast, they are curious and they will try to put absolutely everything into their mouths. Let's consider some of the items around the house that can be poisonous or otherwise dangerous to your puppy.

## UNDER THE MISTLETOE
First, let's look at the plants in your home. The following plants are those most likely to be in your home at holiday time, but the ASPCA's full listing of plants toxic to dogs can be found at www.aspca.org/toxicplants.

Mistletoe is one of the worst offenders at Christmastime. All parts of mistletoe—leaves, stems and berries—are poisonous, but it's the berries that are the most dangerous. Mistletoe berries can be fatal if your puppy ingests even a few. Play it safe and buy a nice artificial cluster. They look quite real, and they eliminate

## CHRISTMAS TREE CAUTION

If you have an overly curious canine when it comes to your Christmas tree, you may want to keep your dog (and your tree) out of harm's way by putting a gate around the tree or otherwise making it inaccessible to your pooch. If your dog chews on the tree or decorations, he could swallow sharp pine needles or ornament hooks, or he could even get electrocuted if he chews on the lights and wires. The tree water can be dangerous, too, especially if you put any type of fertilizer or plant food in it to prolong the life of your tree. At the very least, it can harbor bacteria.

one potential source of trouble. If you positively must have the real thing, make sure it's well out of reach of the puppy, and keep an eye out for any berries that may fall. If your puppy is vomiting, has diarrhea, has seizures or falls into a coma, get him to your veterinarian immediately.

Holly berries can cause upset stomach, seizures and loss of balance, so again, play it safe and invest in some artificial holly. It will last longer, and you can use it again next year.

Poinsettias have always gotten a bad rap as being poisonous, but they're not nearly as bad as mistletoe and holly. The leaves, stems and sap can cause irritation, and if the sap gets in the eyes, it can cause blindness. If your puppy chews on a poinsettia, he could suffer from vomiting and diarrhea. You don't have to eliminate poinsettias from your decorating scheme, but put them in the center of a table, on a mantel or somewhere out of reach of a curious pup. Again, there are some lovely artificial ones on the market.

*What mischief awaits Polo
underneath the Christmas tree?*

*Four-month-old Shenzi picked a prime spot for Santa watching.*

I have never known anyone to decorate for Christmas with these next plants, but, on the off chance that you do, you should know that they don't make good toys for puppies. In fact, if I had a new puppy, I wouldn't even bring boxwood or yew into the house. Boxwood can cause heart failure, and yew has both poisonous berries and foliage. Eating the berries can cause cramping and vomiting. Eating the foliage can cause sudden death, with no symptoms.

The Christmas rose can cause vomiting and diarrhea as well as affect the heart. Last, but not least, ivy can cause vomiting, diarrhea, muscular spasms and paralysis.

## ALSO WATCH OUT FOR . . .

Antifreeze is a good thing when it's in your car, preventing your radiator from freezing. It's a bad thing if your puppy drinks some. Antifreeze has a sweet taste, so dogs think it's a yummy treat, but it's not. It can be fatal if your puppy gets even a tablespoon of it. Symptoms include vomiting, depression, seizures and coma. If you suspect your puppy has swallowed some antifreeze, get him to the vet immediately.

I love kerosene lamps at Christmas. I generally buy the colored lamp oils in red and green and get out my grandmother's old lamps. You can enjoy your kerosene lamps as well. Just remember to keep the kerosene supply locked away from curious canines. If your puppy gets into the kerosene, don't encourage vomiting, as the kerosene will just do more damage to the esophagus and may also get into the lungs. Get him to the vet. If some kerosene spills and puppy gets some on his skin, wash him thoroughly.

**WHAT DO YOU GET . . .**

When you cross a pointer and a setter? A Pointsetter, a traditional Christmas pet.

You'll probably get through the holidays just fine, with no mishaps whatsoever. Take precautions and make sure someone is always watching the puppy when he's not crated.

*Papillon Oliver is looking handsome amid the Christmas décor.*

# Baby, It's Cold Outside

6

## CRATE SWEET CRATE

And now, because it's such an essential tool in house-training, let's begin by talking about that crate we've been mentioning. Getting a crate is one of the most important things you can buy, besides the puppy. I heard that gasp. You're thinking jail, aren't you? Well, don't. A crate becomes your puppy's den, his safe space, where no one bothers him and all is calm. Think playpen or crib if that helps, but not jail. A crate also keeps your puppy safe when you can't watch him or when he might get stepped on or trip someone.

At mealtimes, party times or when no one is home, pop your puppy into his crate. He can't trip anyone, he can't scoot out an open door and he can't chew the fringe on the Persian rug, gnaw on the corner of a wrapped present or, worse, teethe on an electrical cord. If he has an accident, it's in a small, easy-to-clean area, not in the middle of the wall-to-wall carpeting. Get your puppy used to a crate now, and if he ever needs to stay at the vet's office, one of their cages won't seem so strange. He'll also travel easily in the car while in a crate, and many motels and hotels are much more willing to let a dog stay if they know he will be crated in the room.

Besides providing a safe place for your puppy and making a wonderful bed, a crate is indispensable as an aid in house-training. Given a choice, no dog wants to soil his bed, and your puppy is no exception. This doesn't mean that you can just put your puppy in his crate and forget about him. It means that in between trips outdoors and play sessions, the crate provides a haven and helps teach your puppy that he will be taken out at regular intervals.

Crates come in a variety of materials, including lightweight travel crates made of mesh. I don't recommend one of those for a puppy; save that style for an older dog who won't try to chew his way through the mesh. Plastic crates offer protection from drafts and are cozier than wire crates, but they can be too warm in the summer. If you live in a hot climate or your puppy has a very short nose, a wire crate may be a better choice. You can always cover the crate with a blanket or large towel to block drafts and make things snug or take the blanket off to let the air circulate.

There are also stylish crates that blend with formal décor and come with matching beds. Whatever your choice, buy a crate that is sturdy and well made. It may seem like an expensive purchase, but you'll only make it once. Well, okay, you may find that a crate is so indispensable that you'll want more than one, but the point is that they last forever.

I once had three dogs and twelve crates. I've trimmed down a bit. I now have two dogs and six crates. There are two crates in the car for travel and two lightweight mesh crates for taking in and out of motel rooms when we travel. The other two crates flank our bed and double as nightstands. They provide lots of surface, and the dogs enjoy sleeping close to us. You may not want to use crates as tables, but trust me, you will want to use a crate to help train your puppy and to give him a room of his own.

## OH, THE WEATHER OUTSIDE . . .

If you live in Hawaii, Southern California, the South or the Southwest, cold weather may not be an issue, but if you're in another area of the country and you get a Christmas puppy, it's likely to be cold outside. Even if your puppy has a thick, woolly coat, he won't be able to stand as much cold as an adult dog. He may need a puppy coat or sweater if he's going to be outdoors for a play session. Breeds with short coats will need some protection, and even a puppy with lots of hair can get wet and chilled. Puppies don't have the body mass to keep themselves as warm as adult dogs. Limit outdoor time when it's colds and invest in a doggy sweater if you need to. Depending on your puppy's size, a doll's sweater or a

*Staffordshire Bull Terrier buddies in their holiday finery: Spike, Mac and Ele.*

baby sweater will work. Carefully put your puppy's forelegs into the arms of the sweater, and button it over his back. Even if your puppy seems just fine dashing through the snow, don't leave him unattended. Bitter cold can lead to frostbite on paws, noses and the tips of ears and tails.

Why all this talk about weather? House-training won't wait for spring. If you live where there's snow and cold, or if winter means rain every day, be prepared to go out into that cold, snow and rain with your puppy six to ten times a day. For those of you in milder climates, house-training may be a more pleasant experience. Regardless of where you live, though, house-training must begin right away with your new puppy.

House-training will progress rapidly if you establish a schedule and if you designate a specific area of the yard as the "potty zone" to which you always take your puppy to relieve himself. If you don't have a yard, choose a spot on the curbside. Carry your puppy to the desired spot, have him on a lead and don't distract him. This is not the time for a game. After he's done, praise him lavishly, and then you can have some playtime either in the yard or back in the house.

The good news about getting a puppy during the holidays is that there may be more family members home to help share in the house-training duties. Just make sure that, with so many helpers, everyone doesn't think

**BUNDLE UP**

Some pups may be reluctant to go outside in winter weather, depending on breed and size. Toy dogs and lean breeds are especially sensitive to the cold. Consider a doggie sweater and even booties to keep him comfortable during potty trips.

*Cavalier puppies are blooming at Christmastime.*

that someone else is taking care of the puppy. It might be a good idea to make a chart that outlines the puppy's potty schedule and who is responsible for taking the puppy out at what times. The same goes for feeding. Puppies need their regular meals, but they don't need them twice at each mealtime!

Another thing to remember is that your puppy will learn by repetition. Make sure everyone uses the same door to take the puppy in and out. Don't use the side door one time and the sliding door to the deck another time. Be consistent! Otherwise, your puppy will be confused, and house-training will take longer. Believe me, when the wind chill is 20 below zero and the snow is three feet deep, you don't want house-training to take longer.

And speaking of deep snow, you may need to keep puppy's potty area shoveled or tamped down. He'll need a solid place to stand, and you don't want to set him down and have him sink into a snowdrift.

*All of the excitement has left nine-month-old Newfoundland Rudder in need of a nap.*

House-training means taking the puppy out every time you think he needs to go, and he'll need to go a lot. You'll need to take him out after naps, after feeding, after play sessions and anytime in between that your puppy looks as if he's going to "go." Here's what a typical day might look like (make note that you should play with the puppy only *after* he relieves himself so that he learns what his trips outside are for):

> **7 a.m.:** Take the puppy out. Put him in his crate and feed him. Get dressed and take the puppy out again. Play with the puppy for a while (indoors if it is cold). Take him out again. Put him in his crate and have your own breakfast.

> **10 a.m.:** Take the puppy out. Play with the puppy. Take the puppy out and then put him in his crate for a nap. You can use this time to make cookies, run errands or decorate.

**Noon:** Take the puppy out. Feed the puppy. Take the puppy out. Play with the puppy. Put him in his crate.

**3 p.m.:** Puppy out. Playtime. Puppy in crate.

**5 p.m.:** Puppy out. Feed the puppy. Take the puppy out again. Playtime, then crate.

**7 p.m.:** Puppy out.

**9 p.m.:** Puppy out

**11 p.m.:** Puppy out for (hopefully) the final time.

This schedule is just to give you an idea. Puppies, like babies, need lots of sleep to help them grow, so it's likely that your puppy will curl up and nap between outdoor sessions and play periods. Each puppy is an individual. If the family is watching television in the evening and the puppy is content to sleep beside someone's foot or in someone's lap, there's no need to crate him. Just be alert, because when he wakes up he'll have to go.

Some puppies seem to have limitless energy and will only settle down in a crate. We once had a puppy that just didn't know when to quit. As long as he was loose, he was busy. He needed to be put into his crate before he would calm down and nap. If you have that kind of a puppy, make sure that you do put him in his crate for frequent naps.

If you're lucky, that 11 p.m. trip outdoors will be the last of the night and your puppy will

*Golden Retriever Sienna knows that there's no place like home for the holidays.*

*Cold-nosed puppy Mariah doesn't mind the snow.*

sleep until morning. Don't count on being lucky. Young puppies may not be able to hold it overnight, and that means a middle-of-the-night trip outdoors. Again, the crate keeps your puppy confined, and since he won't want to relieve himself in the crate, he'll whine to let you know it's time to go out. Moving your crate to the bedroom or having a second crate there increases your chances that you'll hear the puppy and be able to get him outdoors more quickly, which helps in the house-training process. The fewer accidents your puppy has indoors, the faster he'll learn to always go outdoors.

For the first couple of weeks with your puppy, consider sleeping in a sweat suit so you're ready for action. Or keep a pair of slacks nearby, ready to pull on. Depending on the climate, keep a jacket or coat nearby as well. Get suited up before you take the puppy out of the crate. If you have to put the puppy down to get your coat on, he'll go before you can pick him up again. Keep your boots or shoes near the door so you can slip your feet into them on your way out. Keep his leash near the door as well so you can put it on the puppy as you're going out.

Once you've taken your puppy from the crate, carry him through the house and out the door. Don't open the crate and expect him to follow you through the house. He will squat and go at the first opportunity; with puppies, that means instantly.

Carry your puppy to the designated area in the yard, praise him for going in the right spot and then return to the house. With practice, you'll barely wake up. Here's a tip: making sure your puppy is warm will cut down on nighttime excursions. If your puppy gets cold, he'll wake up, and if he wakes up, he'll have to go.

## THE GREAT INDOORS

Using the great outdoors for house-training is the easiest and simplest method, but there are other ways to do it, and these might have more appeal in the middle of winter. You can combine taking your puppy outdoors with paper training. Choose a room with a washable floor, like a kitchen, laundry room or bathroom, and cover the entire floor with several layers of paper. Put a baby gate in the doorway to confine the pup

### HOLD THE SALT

Be careful where your puppy walks outdoors. Salt used to melt ice and snow can irritate his pads and can cause stomach upset if he licks it off his feet. Wipe his feet after every trip outdoors.

to this room and supply a crate or other bed, a water bowl and toys for your puppy. When your puppy "goes," remove the top layers of paper. It won't take long before your puppy, guided by his excellent sense of smell, catches on that he should go in the same spot he used before. As he learns to go in that particular spot, gradually make the area covered by paper smaller and smaller. If you intend for your dog to go outdoors, continue to take your puppy out whenever possible, maybe using the papers only overnight or when everyone is out for the afternoon.

Eventually you can either take some of that paper out into the yard to help make the transition from indoors to

*Nine-week-old Lily jingles all the way in her red ruff with holiday bells.*

outdoors or, if you have a small dog, you can designate an area indoors as your dog's permanent bathroom. You should clearly define the area; you may want to build a small frame to contain the papers.

If you live in a high-rise building or don't have much of a yard and you've chosen a small dog, you may find it easier to just train your puppy to a certain area of your home, like a corner of a laundry room or possibly an area of a balcony or a patio. Puppies, like cats, can learn to use a litter box. Some doggie litter boxes use sod or artificial turf, while others use dog litter. Dog litter doesn't fly around as much

*It's lovely weather for a sleigh ride with Angel.*

as cat litter does, so if you decide on a litter box, use litter especially made for dogs.

For litter-box training, confine your puppy in one room or area. Surround the litter box with papers, and sprinkle a thin layer of litter over the papers. Gradually reduce the area covered with papers until only the litter box is left. Or, instead of confining the pup to one room, you can use your crate as described earlier, instead of carrying your puppy outdoors, carry him to the litter box. Just remember that the litter box is not a play area. If your puppy starts to play or dig in the litter, remove him, crate him and try again in a little while.

If you decide on a litter box, besides scooping regularly, you will need to empty the box completely, scrub it clean and refill it with fresh litter at least once a week. While you never want to clean up with an ammonia-based product after an accident because it will lure the puppy back to that spot, cleaning a litter box with such a product is a good idea, as it reinforces that the litter box is the place to go.

If you have a small dog and won't be letting him outside for bathroom breaks, washable puppy pads are another alternative. These pads are used instead of litter or paper and can be washed up to about 300 times before they wear out. Pads need to air dry, so you'll need spares. They come in 2 x 2-foot, 3 x 3-foot and 4 x 4-foot sizes.

*Ten-week-old Border Collie Bella lives up to her name in her pink Christmas coat.*

## CLEAN-UP TIME
### Outdoors

Outdoor clean-up is easier with pooper scoopers, which consist of a dustpan like arrangement at the end of one long pole and a small shovel or rake at the end of another pole. No matter how small the dog, you'll want to keep your yard picked up to prevent mess, flies and odor. If your dog relieves himself by the curbside, you will have to clean up immediately every time he defecates. Dispose of the waste in a small garbage can lined with a trash bag. If you live in a climate where the ground doesn't freeze, you can install a doggy septic tank. This fits into a hole dug into the ground, and you deposit the waste into the tank. Enzyme tablets help break down the waste products, and they leach into the soil. If the ground in your yard freezes, you're back to scooping.

Once your puppy is a bit older, you'll likely take him for walks around the neighborhood. Just because it's not your yard doesn't mean you don't have to pick up whatever your puppy leaves behind. Even though it's Christmas, no one wants that kind of "gift." So always carry a supply of plastic bags for picking up after your dog. Puppy-size poops can be managed with a plastic sandwich bag unless you've got a St. Bernard or a Great Dane, in which case move on to plastic grocery bags or bread wrappers. It's a great way to recycle. Just be sure to check first that there aren't any holes in the bag.

### Indoors

Indoors, you'll be cleaning up various surfaces. If your puppy has an accident on linoleum or tile, cleaning up is fairly straightforward. As long as your cleaner doesn't contain ammonia, it doesn't make much difference what you use. The same goes for any accidents in a crate. Easy. The problem is that dogs, when given a choice, want carpeting. I don't care how little carpeting there is in a home or how far away from that carpeting the dog is, if the dog has to vomit or needs a potty break, he is going to find the carpeting. I'm convinced that when cavemen started to share their homes with canines, rather than throw up on dirt or leave the cave, the dog headed for the nearest bearskin.

*In a sweatshirt and booties, Raja
is ready to brave the elements.*

So you've got a mess to get off the carpet. First, remove any solids. You may be able to pick them up with a plastic bag, or you may need something else. Dustpans can make a handy shovel. Another good technique is to take a paper plate, fold it in half, crease the fold and use that to scoop vomit or diarrhea. Once you've gotten all the solids up, you need to select the appropriate cleanser.

*Raphael looks dapper in a festive holiday scarf.*

If your puppy has urinated, you'll want to get as much of the liquid out of the rug as possible before applying a cleanser. Use paper towels to soak up the liquid. This may take a bit of time and quite a few paper towels. Maybe one of the things on your gift list should be stock in a paper company.

Once you've gotten the spot as dry as possible, use a cleanser to finish the job and neutralize the odor. Urine-Off is an enzyme product that works well. Oxygen cleansers also do a good job. For soiled spots, use oxygen cleansers. I've also had good luck with hair shampoo and a toothbrush. Finish off with an enzyme cleanser to help neutralize any residual odor.

Most important, take heart in knowing that you won't be cleaning up puddles and piles forever! If you stick to your routine, most dogs get the hang of housetraining fairly quickly.

# Come, They Told Me

## 7

This chapter provides a solid foundation of the commands that every dog should know. There are many more lessons beyond the basics, so for more in-depth training you can read some of the many wonderful training books available, or you can sign up for a class. I like classes because there's an instructor to answer any questions I might have, and the class structure keeps me working.

## SETTING THE RULES

The first step in training your new puppy is to not let bad habits form. This is much easier than trying to correct problems later on. So decide on rules of the house and make sure every member of the family knows and follows these rules. If the family is not consistent, the dog will be confused and won't understand what he's supposed to do.

If you've decided that "no dogs on the furniture" is one of your rules, don't start letting that cute puppy curl up beside you on the sofa. He won't understand why he can't continue the habit when he's a 60-pound adult and shedding. Don't slip tasty treats to the pleading puppy from the table, or you'll have a dog that will watch every bite you take at every meal for the next 12 years or so. In fact, with a large-breed dog, you run the risk of his making the connection very quickly between table and treats, and he may just decide to skip the middleman and help himself directly. If you absolutely must share with the dog, place the scraps in his own bowl.

## LEASH AND COLLAR

Besides setting house rules and getting everyone to obey them, you'll need to get your puppy used to a leash and collar. Your dog doesn't need to walk in a formal "heel" position, but he does need to learn to walk calmly on a loose lead. There are going to be a lot of walks in his future, not to mention trips to the veterinarian, and you'll need to have him under control.

*Peppy's taste in collars is a bit extreme.*

For your puppy, choose a flat buckle collar. For a correct fit, you should be able to slide two fingers between the collar and your puppy's neck. Let your puppy get used to the collar first. Some puppies seem to not even notice the collar, while others will rub along the floor or scratch at the collar, trying to get it off. A puppy of mine once not only removed the collar but also got it

*"We can go out, but the wrapping paper comes too!"*

unbuckled and left it neatly straightened on the floor. I still can't figure out how she did it.

Once your puppy is comfortable wearing his collar, attach a light lead to the collar. Let him drag it around for a while as you supervise. Do not just attach the lead and walk away. The lead could get tangled around something and panic your puppy, or he could get tangled in the lead and injure himself. Now, pick up the end of the lead and walk along with your puppy, keeping the lead slack. Don't try to guide him at all. Just wander around with him, holding the lead.

Encourage him to walk with you by slapping your leg and calling him. Tasty treats are a good way to keep his interest and get him to keep up with you. If your puppy loses interest and starts to wander in a different direction, stop moving. When the lead tightens, he'll look around to see why you're not moving. Start walking again, and he should hurry to catch up. Again, treats should help the process.

## MORE COLLAR CHOICES

Other collar options include training, or choke, collars and head halters. Training collars can be made of either chain or fabric, and they form a loop that tightens around your dog's neck. If you decide you need this type of collar, never ever leave it on your dog when you're not supervising. The ring can get caught on a protruding object, and your dog can choke to death. Don't let your dog play with other dogs while wearing a training collar either, as that ring can get caught on another dog's collar or jaw, and again your dog could choke.

Head halters are a wonderful invention for dogs who tend to pull while on lead. The collar part fits high and tight around the neck, just below the muzzle and behind the ears, and a loop goes over the snout. A note here: these halters are not muzzles. The loop, when fitted properly, fits below the eyes and is loose. A dog should be able to eat, drink, pant and retrieve toys while wearing a head halter.

You may consider a harness for your dog. For some very small dogs, a harness is a good alternative to a collar because it won't cause any pressure at all on fragile necks. A harness lessens your control over a dog, though, and can encourage him to pull.

Unless you're going to be competing in formal obedience, there's no need to worry about your dog's walking in a precise heel position at your left side. You want a dog who will walk on a slack lead, but you don't need precision for a casual walk around the neighborhood.

## TIPS TO GET YOU STARTED

Before you start your training, there are a few things you should keep in mind. First, keep training lessons short. Puppies can be eager to learn, but their attention span is short, and they need playtime and naptime. Four 5-minute lessons throughout the day are better than one 20-minute lesson.

Always end lessons on a successful note. Since "sit" is one of the easiest things to teach a dog, he should master it rather quickly. Once he has, always end your lessons by asking your puppy to sit, since you know that he will do it correctly.

Choose a release word that lets your puppy know that he can stop doing whatever you've asked him to do. Many people use "okay," but the word doesn't matter as long as you say it happily and are consistent. Don't say "okay" today and "very good" tomorrow.

No hitting and no yelling. If you get frustrated, stop training. Take a walk around the block—without your dog. Count to 100. Do just about anything until you can once again approach your dog calmly.

Finally, no matter what you are teaching, be consistent, be patient and try to keep a sense of humor.

## THE BASIC LESSONS
### Sit

Since I've already mentioned that "sit" is easy to teach, let's start there with your puppy. Get a treat and let your puppy sniff your hand. Let him see the treat, and slowly move the treat back over his nose and between his ears. As he lifts his head to follow the movement of the treat, he will sink down into a sit. Immediately tell him that he's wonderful and give him the treat. Don't hold your hand too high as you move it back or the puppy may jump to try to get the treat.

You can work on the sit throughout the day, not just during your lessons. At feeding time, take a piece of kibble and ask your puppy to sit before you put down his food bowl. You're not only teaching him to sit, you're teaching manners as well. Soon he will be sitting at feeding time instead of leaping and jumping for his food.

## TREATS

I like training with food. Most dogs are very food-motivated, so they're going to pay attention when you have a goodie in your hand. You can use bits of kibble, cheese, cooked meat, just about anything that gets your dog's attention. Some dogs will work happily for their normal kibble; other dogs want something special for their efforts. Your treats don't need to be large. In fact, the smaller the better. You want a trained dog, not a fat dog. Think of a pea. Cut it in half. That's about the size of the treats I use with my Corgi, who weighs 25 pounds.

### Come

We all want our dogs to come to us, and the "come" command could even save your dog's life. If your puppy scoots out an open door, you'll want him to return quickly. If he knows the command "come," he will.

First, always, always praise your dog for coming to you. If you're mad at him or you want him to come to you for something he might find unpleasant, like nail clipping or a bath, go and get him. If something bad happens when he comes to you, why would he ever want to? If I knew someone was going to yell at me or make me do something I didn't like when that person asked me to come, I'd stay as far away as possible.

Next, while you're training, never call your dog if you can't enforce the command. If your dog is chasing a rabbit, it won't do any good to start hollering "come!" Chasing the rabbit is going to be much more rewarding than the piece of cheese in your hand, and your dog will be learning that he doesn't have to obey every time.

Start your training indoors and try to eliminate distractions. Get something really tasty as a treat. Say your puppy's name and the word *come*. Use a happy voice and run backward as you call your puppy. The combination of movement, food and a happy voice should have your puppy scampering to you. Praise him and give him the treat. Practice this command at various times during the day. At mealtimes, call your puppy and rattle the kibble in the bowl as an incentive. At playtimes, pick up a favorite toy and encourage him to come and get it.

Once he seems to understand what "come" means, move your training outdoors. Snow and cold may limit the amount of time you can spend outdoors, but lessons should be kept short anyway.

**COME TIP**

You can lay the foundation for the "come" command before doing any real training. Any time you see your pup coming toward you, say the word *come* and greet him with enthusiastic praise. Make it a game so that he always wants to come when called.

*Heidi dresses the part of Santa's little helper.*

Your puppy may be more interested in the great outdoors than in coming to you, so for outdoor training, attach a light line to his collar and let it drag behind him. If he doesn't come the first time you call him, pick up the line and this time, when you call him, gently reel him in. Give him lots of praise and treats for coming, even if you had to help.

Don't call your puppy on;y when it's time to go inside. Call him, praise and treat and then let him go back to playing in the nearest snowdrift. Never leave the line on him when you're not training, as it could get tangled around something and trap your puppy.

As your puppy catches on to what "come" means, start to take hold of his collar when he comes and then give him the treat. Getting close enough to take his collar in your hand becomes part of the deal. If you really need your dog, it's not much use having him come when called if he just snatches the treat on the run and goes back to whatever he was doing.

Mix up how you call your puppy. Don't always just stand in one place. Call your puppy and then turn and run in the opposite direction. Your puppy gets the fun of a game of tag, as well as praise and a treat when he "catches" you. These things all reinforce the idea that the word *come* means good things when he obeys.

## Down

"Down" is another useful command. Combined with "stay," it lets your dog relax, yet it can keep him out of the way when the need arises. A down-stay in the kitchen keeps the dog from being underfoot while dinner is being prepared. A down-stay in the dining room means he's not going from person to person, begging for food.

To teach the down, have your dog sit. Then take a treat, hold it in front of the dog and move it down toward the floor and slightly forward. Your dog should sink into the down position as he follows the treat. I've seen this work, but my experience with short dogs is that they immediately pop up onto all fours to follow the treat. If this happens, keep your hand closed over the treat and leave your hand on the floor. Your puppy may paw at your hand, or even nibble at it, trying to reach the treat. Be patient. Eventually he will lie down. Immediately praise him and give him the treat.

*Charlie goes for an understated
holiday look in a red bandanna.*

### Stay

"Stay" is a useful command that will keep your puppy in one spot until you let him know he can move. "Stay" means that you can open the door to get the mail and your dog won't dash out into the street. I use the "stay" command when I'm taking something from a hot oven and don't want the dogs to get burned. If I break a glass, "stay" keeps curious dogs out of the room until the shards are cleaned up. Besides keeping your dog safe, you can use the "stay" command with the "down" command (down-stay, as mentioned previously) so that your dog can remain in the room while you are eating, entertaining, and the like, and not be in the way.

Begin teaching the stay in an area with no distractions. Put on your dog's collar and lead and have your dog sit beside you, on your left side. Hold the lead in your right hand and extend your left arm, hand open, in front of your dog's nose. Say "Stay" and take one step forward, turning at the same time so that you are now standing in front of your dog, facing him. Return to your position beside him, then praise and treat. Gradually increase the time between giving the command and giving the treat. Start backing up a step or two.

## SHORT AND SWEET

Remember that a puppy's attention span is very short. If he loses interest in training, he won't learn. End the lesson if pup becomes bored, and try again later.

Eventually, add movement before you return to your dog. Give the "stay" command and then walk back and forth in front of your dog. Walk around him to get back into position beside him. Don't rush things. If your dog breaks the stay, just return him to his original position and try again. Once

*All aboard the Christmas Express with Autumn!*

you feel that your dog understands the command, take the lead off (indoors only) and try the same movements as when your dog was on lead. Leave the room for a second or two and return.

Teach the down-stay the same way, but with your dog lying down instead of sitting. To a dog, "stay" when he's sitting is different from "stay" when he's lying down. He may learn the down-stay faster, but it's still a brand-new command for him, so start at the beginning.

### Leave It and Drop It

Trust me, you definitely want to teach these two commands. "Leave it" means "don't touch that slice of onion I just dropped on the floor." "Drop it" means "I know you're proud of that dead squirrel in your mouth, but I'd prefer you left it outside." "Leave it" and "drop it" are much faster to say, and dogs appreciate brevity. They don't need long explanations.

Teaching the pup to drop it is easy. When your puppy has a toy in his mouth, show him a yummy treat and give the command "drop it." When he drops the toy to go after the treat, give him the treat, then pick up the toy and give it back to him. If he has something in his mouth you'd rather he didn't have, like a sock, give the command, give the treat and then give him a substitute for the sock, like a chew stick or a toy. Some people also teach the word *trade*, so that the dog will give up something in exchange for something else.

Both of my dogs know what I mean when I say "drop it," but with my male, that doesn't mean he's going to obey. He learned very quickly what "trade" means, though. If what I want him to drop is something wonder-

*Cairn Terrier Reese was six months old on her first Christmas.*

ful, like his favorite toy, I say "trade" and he runs to the kitchen, drops the object and looks at the treat jar for his reward.

Teach your dog to leave it, and when you drop anything, from a pill to a piece of chicken, you can safely pick it up again before your dog devours it. To teach leave it, get plenty of treats. Take a treat and place it on the floor where you dog can see it. As the dog goes for the treat, cover it with your hand. He may paw and nibble, but eventually he will back off. The minute he does, tell him he's a good dog and give him a treat with your other hand.

When he backs off consistently, uncover the treat on the floor and tell your dog to leave

*Whippet River gives Santa her Christmas wish list.*

it. If he tries to eat it, cover it again. As soon as he actually does leave it, give him the treat in your other hand and pick up the one on the floor.

## CLICKER TRAINING

Throughout this chapter, I've said to praise your dog and offer tasty treats as rewards, but you can also train with a clicker, a small noisemaker that marks the behavior you want from your puppy the minute he does it. The noise is followed by a treat. The advantage to clicker training is that, once you get the hang of it, it lets your dog know immediately when he's done the right thing. The clicker has no "tone of voice," so your own frustration or anger

*Yorkies Kayla and Ruben have the welcome mat out for their holiday guests.*

doesn't get in the way when your dog isn't doing quite the right thing.

You can buy a clicker at a pet-supply store or, if you buy a book on clicker training, it may come with a clicker. The first thing to do is to get your dog used to the sound and teach him that when he hears that sound, a treat will follow. Get your puppy and a bunch of treats. Click the clicker and give him a treat. Do it again. Repeat. After about a dozen clicks and treats, your puppy will know what that sound means, and you're ready to start training.

The three ways people train with clickers are luring, shaping and capturing. To teach your puppy to sit, you lure him into a sit by moving the food over his head as previously described. When he sits, click and treat. When I described how to teach your puppy to lie down, that also was luring.

With shaping and capturing, your dog knows you want him to do something and will actively try to figure out what you want. To shape a behavior, watch your dog and click when he begins to do something you want him to do. For instance, if you want him to jump up onto the sofa, click and treat when he walks near the sofa. Once he's figured out that he gets a treat when he's near the sofa, treat only when he jumps up on it. If you want him to lie down on the sofa, don't click when he's standing on it, but do click first for a sit and then only for a down.

Capturing is clicking only for the final result. For instance, my female would "sit pretty" or "beg" on her own when she wanted something, so I started clicking and treating every time she sat up that way. I named the behavior "circus." Now, when I say "circus," she sits up and looks adorable. Of course, I didn't teach the adorable part; dogs do that on their own.

*A true Christmas pup, Bailey came home to his family on Christmas Eve.*

# Don We Now Our Gay Apparel

8

If there's anything cuter than a puppy, it's a puppy wearing festive attire. It might be a bow, or a pair of antlers or a full Santa suit. Catalogs and pet-supply stores have all kinds of wonderful holiday outfits, and there's always that old standby, a big Christmas bow around the neck. Before we go dressing up puppy for the holidays, though, let's think about what basics he needs in his everyday "wardrobe."

## ESSENTIAL ACCESSORIES

First, consider a flat buckle collar and leash. These items are to a dog as the "little black dress" is to a woman. A collar and leash are basic canine wear. With them, your dog can go anywhere. Of course, puppies grow rapidly, so don't invest in that custom-made leather collar with your dog's name embossed on it just yet. Instead, consider a woven nylon collar designed so that the tongue of the buckle can be pushed through the fabric anywhere. Since there are not specific holes for the buckle, it ensures a customized fit and gives you lots of options to expand the collar as your puppy grows. Plus, it's lightweight and washable. You will also need a lead to

*Boxer Hines is serious about holiday fun.*

go with that collar, one that is appropriate to your pup's size and strength. Most pups will do fine with a lightweight lead. It's nice if the collar and lead are color coordinated, but you can always save that fashion statement for when your dog is fully grown.

Nylon leads and collars offer the most variety in both size and color, and they are also sturdy and long wearing, as well as being washable. Leather collars and leads are also long lasting, and they look nice. Leather leads get suppler with age. However, leather may be more tempting as a chew toy, so until your dog is well beyond the teething stage, keep the lead out of reach. Leather collars and leads can be cleaned with saddle soap. Collars made of cotton web are another good choice, but they don't usually come in as wide a variety of colors.

There are chain leads on the market, but these are not your best choice. The nylon or plastic loops at the end frequently will crack and split. Chain is also overkill. You can manage a dog of any size quite well with a leather, nylon or cotton lead. Another strike against chain is that if you grab the chain as you control your dog and your dog suddenly lunges, that chain dragging across your palms is quite likely to shred a bit of flesh.

If your puppy is already a bit of an escape artist, consider a martingale collar. A martingale collar is usually made of nylon and consists of a large loop that fits around the dog's neck and a smaller loop to which the lead is attached. If the dog pulls or tries to back out of the collar, it tightens around the dog's neck to prevent him from escaping. While the collar does tighten enough so that a dog can't get out of it, it won't choke the dog if fitted properly.

## OUR GAY APPAREL

If you want more than the basics for the holidays and would like your puppy to sport the latest T-shirt, sweater or costume, you'll need to think about some of the same things you'd think about if you were wearing the outfit. Size and comfort head the list, but there's also safety to consider, just as when your kids wear Halloween costumes. Whatever your dog wears should

*Mini Schnauzer Brody celebrates with a friend.*

be flame retardant. There shouldn't be a lot of floppy bits or loops or anything that is likely to snag on furniture or knock things off a table. Besides, even if your puppy doesn't mind the outfit, if he gets caught on something or trapped and can't escape, he's likely to panic and may hurt himself trying to get loose.

Make sure whatever your dog wears fits. If it's too tight, it will make him uncomfortable, and too loose can mean that he gets tangled up and could get hurt. Think about comfort as well. A Santa hat or a pair of antlers may be held on with elastic, which may eventually annoy the puppy. Keep an eye on how your puppy is acting. If he starts to scratch at straps or hats, it's time to let him turn back into a dog.

The same goes for that adorable ribbon around your pup's neck. Not only might it start to chafe, but if your puppy can wiggle it around, he may decide that the bow looks good enough to eat. Ribbon is not meant for a dog's (or anyone's) digestive tract. Avoid emergency surgery by making sure that your puppy's wardrobe does not turn into a snack.

If your particular puppy thinks everything is edible, forgo the costume and simply invest in a red or green puppy collar, with or without a matching lead, for the

## PICTURES WITH SANTA

Some mall Santas will consider having puppies on their laps. Many pet-supply stores and animal shelters also have opportunities to have pets photographed with Santa, with the proceeds going toward helping homeless animals. That could be the perfect solution. You'll have Santa and a photographer and you'll be donating to a good cause.

holidays. Whatever your decision, don't leave your puppy unattended while he is wearing a costume.

## PICTURE PERFECT

Another thing to consider is a puppy Christmas portrait. Get everything all set up for the picture before you add the puppy to the mix. If it's a full family portrait, figure out where everyone is going to be and then go get the puppy. Or, if you think a puppy in a stocking or in a gift box would be cute, practice first without the puppy. Know where you're going to stand or sit to

*Shih Tzu Shodu is the picture of holiday style from head to toe.*

take the picture. Consider the background and remove clutter. Pay attention to light and shadow. Once you're all ready to click the shutter, put the puppy in the stocking or box and take the picture quickly! Puppies are not known for holding still. One tip is to plan the photo session after one of puppy's mealtimes or playtimes, when he is likely to be a bit drowsy and more willing to hold still for a portrait.

Of course, if you're computer literate, you can just take any photo of the puppy and create a Christmas card around the photo, which may be a bit easier than trying to get your pup to sit for a portrait.

## PRETTY PUPPY

If you're not into dressing up your dog, or if he is against the idea, that's okay because a puppy doesn't need accessories to look absolutely adorable. Your guests will take one look and want to cuddle the new family member, which brings us to brushing and grooming. No one is going to want to hug a dirty puppy, and no one is going to be happy if too-long nails snag their Christmas finery.

Grooming a dog is easier if the dog is on your level. A grooming table is ideal because it can be set up easily, has a skid-proof top and is the proper height; but if you don't want to invest in a special grooming table, there are other options. I once used a rubber mat on top of our clothes dryer. You can turn almost any table or

*Toby cuddles up for his photo with Santa.*

countertop into a grooming surface with the addition of a nonskid mat. Rubber bath mats work well, depending on the size of the dog.

Another alternative is a bed. Cover the spread with a sheet, and you can work there. I frequently do this with my older dog, as he can then sit or lie down while I work, and it's nice and soft. You can, of course, work on the floor, but this increases the chance of your dog's getting away from you, and it can turn your back into a pretzel.

Many dogs take offense at having their tootsies touched, so before you ever start trimming nails, get in the habit of touching your puppy's feet every day. Don't be rough, but do get your puppy used to having his feet held. Hold the puppy firmly and then gently clasp a paw. Tasty treats can be used to let the puppy know that good things happen when someone touches his feet.

Depending on the size and age of your puppy, you might be able to use human nail clippers at first. Just snip the sharp tips off each nail. As your puppy grows, you'll need heavier nail clippers made for dogs. Clip where the nail starts to curve, and try to avoid the quick, the blood vessel that runs down the center of each nail. If your puppy has clear nails, you'll be able to see the quick. If your puppy has dark nails, good luck. You will have to take it slowly and clip only a small bit at a time.

You might also consider a grinder. A grinder has a rotating

## DRESSY DOG

Holiday wear for your pup is so much more than reindeer ears these days! Party dresses, fancy coats, jeweled collars and more can be found at pet boutiques and online retailers so that both you and your pup can wear your holiday best.

*Jenny T. is ready for her close-up.*

drum that quickly grinds away the nail. In spite of the noise of the motor, many dogs prefer the grinder, but you'll still want to get your puppy used to it ahead of time. Start by turning on the grinder and letting the puppy get used to the noise. In another session, hold the handle of the grinder against a foot, so the puppy can feel the vibrations. Later still, grind a nail. Stop if your puppy struggles. Give lots of treats during this process. Eventually you'll be able to grind all four feet with a minimum of fuss.

If you just can't seem to manage your dog's nails, no matter what you try, make an appointment with a groomer and have a professional do it. The important thing is that the nails get cut. Besides the fact that long nails can snag on clothing or scratch, long nails cause a dog's feet to spread and also make it hard for a dog to walk.

The type of brushes and combs you'll need will depend on your puppy's coat. If you're unsure, ask a groomer for recommendations. If you have a puppy with a curly coat, like a Poodle or a Bichon Frise, you'll need to groom him more often and may eventually want to just schedule regular grooming sessions with a professional every four to six weeks. That curly coat will need regular brushing out so that it doesn't mat, and, unlike other types of dog coat, that curly coat keeps on growing, just like human hair. So, at the least, you'll need scissors, clippers, a comb and a slicker brush. A slicker brush has wire bristles that are bent at the tip to rake through the coat.

If you have a short-coated dog, like a Beagle or a Dalmatian, consider a hound glove. These are mitts with either a nubby surface or a rough texture that helps loosen and remove all those stubborn little hairs that are just waiting to work their way into your upholstery and carpeting.

Dogs with double coats, that is, a soft cottony layer underneath and a harsher layer on top, will shed noticeably, especially when the undercoat sheds out twice a year. You'll need a comb, a slicker brush and possibly a shedding rake to remove the dead undercoat.

Dogs like Cocker Spaniels and setters will need combing in addition to regular brushing. You can use a metal comb or a slicker brush to gently comb out the feathering on their legs and ears.

Whenever your groom your dog, dampen the coat before brushing. This will help prevent breaking the hair. Add a bit of mouthwash to the water, and it will help remove dust and dirt and leave the dog's coat with a fresh smell.

Brush your dog at least once a week. You don't need to bathe your dog at every grooming session. Too much bathing can strip the coat of essential oils. That's not to say that your dog won't ever need a bath. Many hounds have a protective oily coat that can start to smell "doggy," and a bath can make such a dog nicer to live with. When a heavily coated dog is shedding, a good bath will help loosen the hair and hasten the shedding process. If your dog rolls in something nasty, a bath may be the only answer.

A professional groomer will do a terrific job of bathing your dog, or you can do it yourself. If you choose to bathe your dog at home, first dress in something that you don't mind getting wet. Trust me, you will get wet. Next, get everything ready before you round up

*Elvira's not shy about displaying her holiday spirit.*

the dog. There are wonderful attachments that can turn your bathtub into a doggie spa, or you can use a large pan or unbreakable pitcher to pour water over your dog. Depending on your dog's size, a utility sink can work and is much easier on your back. Put a mat of some kind on the tub or sink bottom so your dog won't slip. If you're using the bathtub, get a cushion or foam pad or several towels as padding for your knees. Have your dog shampoo at hand. Always use dog shampoo, not shampoo made for human hair, for the correct pH for your dog. You may want an old washcloth for wiping off your dog's face, and if you decide to put cotton balls in his ears, have those ready too. Get several towels for drying off the dog.

Brush your dog thoroughly before the bath. This will remove dead hair and untangle any snarls, which will be almost impossible to comb out once they get wet.

Now, pick up your dog or, if that's not possible, put your dog on a leash and lead him into the bathroom. Shut the door to keep your dog from escaping. Run the water to the desired temperature before you put the dog in the tub. You don't want to scald his toes as you adjust the water. Put your dog in the tub. If you want to put cotton balls in his ears to keep water out, now's the time to do so. My experience is that the dog will just shake his head until the cotton flies out. An alternative, if your dog has floppy ears, is to hold your hand over the ear opening as you wash the flap with the other hand. With prick-eared dogs, either fold the ears over or wash the ears with a washcloth and very little soap.

Wash your dog's face with water only, and use a washcloth. If you have a dog with facial wrinkles, clean the wrinkles carefully, and make sure they are completely dry after the bath or you risk the growth of bacteria in all those folds.

Now, wet your dog all over by using a shower extension or pouring water over the dog. Pour on some shampoo and work the lather into the coat. Don't miss the armpits, tummy and paws. Rinse. Repeat the sudsing. Rinse again. Some vinegar in the rinse water will help cut the suds and add shine to the coat. Make sure you get all of the soap out of the coat, or your dog will be scratching at itchy soap residue. Take care to not get soap in your dog's eyes. If you have a dog with protruding eyes, be especially careful.

Once your dog is rinsed, don't take him out of the tub immediately. Wait a minute and see whether he'll shake. It will save you a lot of mopping up if he shakes himself off in the tub instead of all over the bathroom or elsewhere in the house. You'd be amazed at how much water even a short coat can hold. Then, wrap your dog in a towel and lift or guide him out of the tub. Don't let your dog leap out on his own; he could get hurt. Use as many towels as you need to get your dog dry. If you're bathing in warm weather, you can let your dog air dry, although if you have a dog like a Poodle, you will need to brush the hair dry, or it will dry in very tight little curls and may start to mat. If you're bathing in cold weather, don't let your dog outside until he is totally dry. This may mean that you'll need to use a hair dryer.

If you'll be doing enough bathing to make it worthwhile, invest in a dog dryer. If you decide to use your own hair dryer, put it on "air only" if it has such a setting. If not, use the lowest possible setting and keep the dryer moving. Never hold it in one spot, or it will burn your dog's skin. As you dry the coat, use a brush to allow the air to reach the base of the fur.

When you finally let your dog outside, don't be surprised if he rolls on the ground. Just hope he chooses grass, not the nearest mud hole.

Don't forget your dog's teeth. True, dog teeth are not the same as human teeth, so your puppy is not likely to get cavities, but plaque and tartar can build up on a canine's canines, and that can be a problem. Dog breath will never be a wonderful smell, but a dirty mouth will smell even worse and can mean bacteria, which can compromise your dog's health.

Make it a habit to brush your dog's teeth. Three times a week is good, but even once a week is better than nothing. Get your puppy used to your rubbing his teeth with your finger. A dab of liverwurst can make

*Groomed and ready for the holidays, Bailey's looking good.*

it a pleasant experience. Cover your finger with a piece of gauze and gently go over the teeth. Once your puppy is comfortable with that, you can graduate to a dog toothbrush and dog toothpaste. Never use human toothpaste on your dog; the fluoride in the toothpaste can make him sick.

Your dog may also need a professional dental cleaning. Your vet will advise you. Some dogs build up tartar faster than others. My male needs professional cleanings twice a year; my female hasn't needed one yet, and she's five years old.

The holidays can offer some great ideas for naming your new addition. The obvious choices are the reindeer names: Dasher, Dancer, Prancer, Vixen, Comet, Cupid, Donner and Blitzen. Rudolph is another thought, or even Olive, from *Olive, the Other Reindeer*. Other animated holiday specials might mean that your puppy becomes a Herbie, Clarice or Nestor.

Maybe you'll choose Noel, Yule, Merry, Carol, Star or Gift. Or how about Nick, for St. Nicholas? If your puppy is white, you could borrow from the weather, with Snowflake, Blizzard or Drift. Stormy and Frosty are other considerations. You might like the name Angel, or something from a Christmas carol. A male dog could easily be Herald or King. Holly and Ivy would both work for females. A black dog could be Midnight. And there's always Tinsel and Garland for pups with particularly sparkling personalities. As a nod to Chanukah, I think Dreidel would make a terrific name for a busy puppy who spins like a top.

I'm rather fond of the 1954 movie *White Christmas*, so I might consider Bing or Clooney as names for a holiday pup. A friend has a passion for

*Lucky and Shadow reenact How the Grinch Stole Christmas during their first Christmas together.*

Handel's *Messiah* and thinks Emmanuel is a great choice. He's also mentioned Wonderful! And Counselor! They might work, but I'd feel as if I had to sing those names, and given my talents at singing that could lead to a charge of disturbing the peace.

Take a look around the holiday kitchen and maybe you'll be inspired. Pumpkin, Spice, Pepper, Ginger, Cinnamon, Clove, Nutmeg, Currant, Raisin, Cookie, Chipper, Cocoa, Fudge, Penuche and Candy might all be good names. What about Eggnog or Sugarplum? I suppose you could call a dog Fruitcake or Turkey, but that doesn't seem very complimentary to me.

Possibly your Christmas tradition includes an ethnic food or tradition that could lend itself to being a puppy's name. My hometown is predominately Swedish and Italian, and both of those cultures have all kinds of food as a way to celebrate Christmas. Lutfisk is dried cod, which might not have a lot of appeal, but the word "lutfisk" isn't too bad. Korv is a type of sausage, so maybe it's a good name for a Dachshund?

Some of my research of Italian goodies had me drooling and wishing for Christmas! In medieval times sugared almonds, or treggea, were a common treat, as was confetti, or sugarcoated whole spices. I've enjoyed zeppole and struffoli, which are fried treats similar to a doughnut. Pandoro is a sweet bread filled with spices, nuts and dried fruits. Certainly I'd rather call a dog Pandoro than Fruitcake!

*Matilda (Tilly) relaxes at home for the holidays.*

*Molly Jo's Christmas card photo is picture perfect.*

Two Polish names I like are Piernik, which is a honey cake, and Uszka (USH-kah), a holiday dumpling. You don't have to choose a holiday name, of course, but it is a great way to commemorate getting your puppy at Christmas.

Another idea is to consider your own heritage or your dog's heritage when naming your dog. If you have an Irish Wolfhound, find a Celtic name. I've given several of my Pembroke Welsh Corgis names with a Welsh origin. If you're Scottish, there may be a family name that will be just right for your puppy.

Sports fans frequently choose the names of players on their favorite teams. Sometimes people choose names that are the opposite of what a person might think when seeing the dog. For instance, Bruiser or Killer for a Chihuahua or Baby or Tiny for a Great Dane.

Whatever name you finally select, there are a couple of things to keep in mind. First, make sure the entire family is in agreement. Otherwise, if someone doesn't like the name, he may never use it, calling the dog by some other name, which could confuse the dog. Or a person who doesn't like the name might never say it in a happy tone of voice. Growing up, my first dog was a Collie. When the topic of naming her came up, my father said, "Anything but Lassie."

## A TASTY LESSON

You can easily teach puppy his name. Use a treat that you can break into tiny pieces. Say his name and reward him with a bit of the treat when he looks at you. Repeat about ten times, and do this several times a day. It won't take long for him to respond every time you say his name.

Another point to consider is that the name should be easy to say. You're going to be calling your dog by that name for 12 to 18 years, so this is not the time for a tongue twister. You should also remember that if you're outside calling your dog, your neighbors will probably hear you. Naming a dog Firebird or Firecracker might sound wonderful, but if you shorten that name to Fire, you could get in trouble hollering "Fire!"

I have a friend with a dog, and the kids named it Smooch. The name fits the dog, but I'm not sure I'd want to be hollering "Smooch" at the top of my lungs

*"I'm ready to help pull Santa's sleigh!"*

every day. I have another friend who says he would hate to have to call his neighbor's dog, who's called Precious. For the same reason, stay away from something you think is funny or something that's off color. The novelty of such a name will wear thin. Pick a name you'll be comfortable with in public for at least a decade to come.

*(left) to (right): Becky, Lucy and Chester are a happy holiday trio.*

## SING WE NOW OF CHRISTMAS

In his book *Merle's Door*, Ted Kerasote says that his dog Merle, on their first Christmas together, howled along with the Hallelujah chorus of Handel's *Messiah*. "As its opening bars sounded, he threw himself to his feet, eyes stunned with wonder and disbelief. Tossing back his head . . . he caroled along . . . his mouth nearly coming unhinged . . . until the monumental final chords when—voice cracking and tail lashing—he looked up at me with an angelic and spent expression, as if to say, 'That is the most sublime music I have ever heard.'"

# Say Hello to Friends You Know

There may be drawbacks to getting a puppy during the holidays, but one thing is certain: the holidays offer plenty of opportunities to socialize your pet. Socialization is as important as good food, a house-training schedule and a warm bed. It means your puppy will meet lots of friendly people of all kinds and will accept people as friends. You don't want your puppy overwhelmed, but you do want him to know that people come in all shapes and sizes and wear all kinds of different things and that there's nothing to fear.

Dogs are social animals. They enjoy being around other dogs and people, but they need to learn that strangers aren't scary. Your puppy accepts the family as part of his "pack," and now he needs to learn that other people can be part of an extended pack and that he doesn't have to be afraid.

Keeping in mind that puppies need lots of rest and that you don't want to overwhelm the puppy, there are still many opportunities for positive social interaction. If you have children, have them invite their friends over (as if you could stop them!). Dogs seem to view adults and children as two totally separate species (and anyone with

*Christmas cutie Jenna Blu, a six-month-old Yorkie.*

teenagers would probably agree!). Children tend to move more quickly, and their movements are jerkier. Their voices are higher and, when they're excited or playing, may be quite shrill. Puppies need to learn early that these movements are not a threat and, more important, that those shrill noises are not the noises of prey.

Never leave an infant and a dog alone together. Always supervise. Baby noises, especially, can trigger predatory behavior. That doesn't mean that your puppy shouldn't meet the baby. Most dogs seem to understand that babies are helpless, and many dogs will feel quite protective, but you don't want to take a chance.

If you don't have children of your own, well, school's out, so find some. Ask the neighbors if their children can come over to meet the puppy. Take a short walk down the block when you see children outside. Trust me, your puppy needs contact with children.

Your puppy will meet adults if you have friends and relatives in for an eggnog or two or if you're hosting Christmas dinner this year. Again, don't overwhelm the puppy, but do let guests and puppy say hello to each other before you crate the puppy.

If you've got the time and energy, a shopping mall can be a wonderful place to socialize a puppy. There will be lots of people and quite possibly strollers and wheelchairs. It's important that your puppy meets men and women, adults and children, people wearing glasses, people wearing hats, and so on. If you have a friend with a beard, introduce him to your puppy. It's amazing what dogs can notice—and bark at. If you can offer your puppy a new experience every day, you'll come a long way in creating a friendly, confident adult dog.

Remember, though, don't force any of these new experiences on your dog. Let your puppy approach strangers at his own pace. If he's getting tired or seems fearful, give him a time out. Pop him in his crate for a nap or end the session at the mall. Puppies, like babies, have short attention spans and need lots of sleep.

Don't forget other animals when you're socializing. If you have an older dog, odds are good that he and the puppy will get along just fine. I've never had a problem introducing a new puppy to my older dogs, but I do use caution. Make the introductions out in the yard, if possible,

*Buster (left) and Buddy (right) are happy
to lend a paw with the decorations.*

*Llord Armani has a festive holiday greeting for visitors.*

rather than in the house. If the yard is securely fenced, the puppy can be off leash, but put your older dog on a leash and keep the leash slack. A tight leash translates as tension and can make your dog wonder what the problem is. Don't leave the dogs alone and don't let the puppy be a pest.

Indoors, feed the dogs in separate areas so there's no arguing over food. Feeding the puppy in his crate is a good idea. That way, the older dog can't steal the puppy's food, and the puppy can't annoy the older dog while he's eating.

Don't ignore the older dog in favor of the puppy. Take the time to give him some love and have a play session just for him, without the bratty puppy chewing on his ears or tail. Let him keep his toys; if he's got a favorite, don't make him share it with the puppy. That could lead to ill feelings. If you give the puppy a treat, give one to the older dog as well.

If you don't have another dog, see whether there's a friendly dog in the neighborhood who might make a good playmate. Try to match sizes. A much bigger dog might be perfectly friendly and willing to play, but he might also accidentally harm a small puppy. If someone else in the neighborhood also got a puppy, so much the better. Arrange some play dates either indoors or in a securely fenced area outdoors. You don't want a puppy darting out into the street.

Another great way to socialize a puppy with both people and other dogs is a puppy kindergarten class. Check with local dog trainers, animal shelters and boarding kennels to see whether they offer classes. Puppy kindergarten classes are just for socialization. They teach your puppy that good things happen when strangers are around. There's lots of petting and lots of treats. Puppies also get to play with other puppies their size, helping them develop a good attitude around strange dogs.

Cats and dogs can get along well together, but if you have a resident cat, it may take some time before that cat fully accepts a boisterous puppy, especially if the puppy is the first dog in the household. First, make sure that your cat has places she can go to escape from the puppy. Clear off the mantel or a bookshelf. Use baby gates. Most cats can leap over them; most puppies can't. Put your cat's food and water dishes somewhere out of reach of the puppy. Do the same with the litter box. Your cat should be able to relieve herself without being bothered by a puppy, and puppies, indeed even adult dogs, seem to find the contents of litter boxes tasty. Eeeww.

Take introductions slowly. Put your puppy in his crate and let the cat approach the crate. Contain your puppy in an exercise pen and let the cat get as close as she feels comfortable

## SOCIABLE AND SAFE

With guests stopping by and general hustle and bustle in the household, be sure to keep an eye on your pup! Make sure he doesn't scurry out the front door as guests are coming and going, and make sure that someone doesn't inadvertently leave an off-limits puppy area ungated or with the door open.

# Puppy's First Christmas

*Boxer pup Zachary is his family's favorite Christmas present.*

doing. Praise both the cat and the puppy and offer treats when they approach each other calmly, with no growling or hissing.

If you have other pets, like rabbits, guinea pigs, hamsters or gerbils, they are probably not going to become bosom buddies with your dog. These small animals are more likely going to be considered lunch by your dog. Keep small furry pets safe in their cages, up on shelves, and, if possible, in a room with the door shut. Sure, we've all seen pictures of the mouse sitting on a dog's head or a rabbit curled up between a dog's front paws, but these are exceptions. Generally, your dog won't consider these animals as pals, but as prey.

Socialization opportunities include new experiences as well as meeting new friends. Get your puppy used to objects and noises as well as people and other animals. Don't isolate your puppy, but let him spend the day in a busy room, where he'll get used to televisions and radios as well as the ring of a doorbell or a telephone. If he's kept in the kitchen, he'll soon get used to pots and pans rattling and the buzz of a timer or microwave. Encourage him to approach strange objects. Praise him if he smells them. If something seems to scare him, don't force him to approach, but you can coax him with treats until he discovers for himself that there's nothing to fear. I teach all my puppies to "smell" or "sniff" and praise them for doing so. This way, even if something is new, they

**PLEASED TO MEET YOU**

Socialization is a good thing, but don't let pup get overwhelmed. And make sure that everyone who handles your puppy does so properly, not agitating or frightening him.

*Barely big enough to reach the pedals, Chihuahua pup Peanut takes a Christmas joy ride.*

are willing to approach and check it out because they know they'll get a reward.

Get your puppy used to riding in your car. During your dog's lifetime, he'll need to ride in the car to the veterinarian's, and there may be trips to the boarding kennel or even longer rides on family vacations. Most puppies adjust easily to riding in the car, but some may get carsick at first. Keep initial rides short and happy, gradually increasing the length, and carry a roll of paper towels for clean-up. And don't have every ride end at the vet's. How eager would you be to get in a car if every ride ended at the doctor's office?

The ride doesn't have to have a destination. You can just drive around the block a few times and return home. Or take the puppy with you when you run errands, as long as you don't have to leave him in the car. Just remember that a cold car in the winter can be as dangerous as a hot car in the summer.

When you do take your puppy for a ride, don't let him ride loose. Besides risking a puddle or two on your car's upholstery, a loose puppy in the car can be dangerous. Puppies like to scoot into small spaces, and that space between the gas and brake pedals may really appeal to him. If he's on the seat with you or in your lap, you may find yourself paying more attention to the puppy than to your driving. Another reason to restrain your puppy is that if there's an accident, your puppy can become a flying object.

Crate your puppy in the back seat; use a sturdy plastic crate to protect your puppy in case of an accident. Once he's grown up a bit, and depending on his size, you might want to get him a car seat. This type of seat boosts your dog up so he can see out the window and is secured in place with the regular seat belt. There are also harnesses available that enable you to strap your dog in the same way as with a seat belt. Whatever system you decide on for restraint, use something to keep your puppy safe.

*Carriage dogs through and through, Dalmatians Pongo and Rorschach are ready to roll.*

# OF
# TREES AND
# DOGS AND GIFTS

Dogs can enjoy Christmas as much as
people, but their way of celebrating and
ours may not be the same. A tree indoors
can be quite a temptation to a male dog, and
especially to a puppy who is still trying to figure
out the rules and just where he can and can't go.
Dog owner and writer Lexiann Grant says that
her Norwegian Elkhound Wylie, at age 11
months, showed his approval of his first
Christmas tree by raising his leg as high as
it would go and watering the tree.

Another year, Lexi's young Afghan Hound, ignoring the fact that Christmas is a time of sharing, ate an entire 12-pound turkey all by herself. Her dogs have not limited themselves to turkey. Libbet, a Norwegian Buhund, stole a figurine from the manger scene and chomped it to pieces. Another dog, Oslo, also couldn't resist the manger scene: he ate half a camel, a donkey ear and two legs from a lamb. Talk about indigestion!

Wylie left the crèche alone but did enjoy removing and chewing the felt ornaments from an Advent calendar. He and Oslo then teamed up so that Oslo could have his share of the fun. Oslo would stare at a particular ornament on the tree and Wylie would take it off the tree and give it to Oslo. I guess her dogs know the meaning of sharing after all.

Veterinarian Jill Richardson adopted a young Neapolitan Mastiff just before Christmas one year, and the dog fell in love with the tree. He slept under it and used his hind legs to shove all the packages out of the way. Jill says she left the tree up long after Christmas because he enjoyed it so much.

Dena Harris noted a bit of favoritism when her parents got a puppy. She reports that the puppy got a stocking that was twice as large as any human's, that the puppy got to open his stocking first, and that the majority of the day's video recording was of the puppy.

It's not just puppies that enjoy Christmas. As your dog grows, so will the traditions that get added each year. Your dog is part of the family, so it's only natural that you'll include him in your celebrations.

Gail Parker of Philadelphia has Irish Setters, and not only do they all get gifts from her but Gail and her friends also make sure that all of their dogs exchange gifts. She calls UPS "United Puppy Service."

Of course, dogs being dogs, just a pile of wrapping paper can be a wonderful toy. Puppies, especially, won't need special gifts. Just throw the shredded paper in a heap and let your puppy finish the destruction. Keep ribbons out of the mix so your puppy doesn't get tangled up or choke, and make sure that he doesn't actually eat the paper. Oh, sure, there may be the minor possibility that tearing up the wrapping paper will teach the puppy to tear up other kinds of paper, but come on, it's Christmas. Lighten up!

## CHOOSING A VET

If you already have a pet or two, then you've already got a veterinarian you rely on. If this puppy is your first pet, then you'll need to choose a veterinarian, and sooner is much better than later. Choose your vet now, before you get your puppy, not when you're faced with a life-threatening emergency in the middle of the night.

If you have friends or neighbors who have pets, they are a good place to start in your search for a vet. Ask which veterinarian they use, and why. Ask what they especially like or dislike about the practice. Consider your own preferences as well. For instance, your neighbors may praise a veterinarian in the next town, but you may feel comfortable having a vet close by for convenience or in case of an emergency.

Think about whether you want a large practice with several vets or a smaller office with just one vet. The advantage of a small office is that the same vet will see your dog every time you visit. He'll know you and your dog. On the down side, if there's an emergency and you need to take your dog to another clinic, no one will know your dog's medical history. In a multivet

*Mocha sends an adorable Christmas greeting.*

practice, you may not get to know each doctor as well, but every vet will have access to your dog's file in an emergency.

Speaking of emergencies, in your search for a veterinarian, ask how the office handles emergencies. Is there an answering service? Does your vet share after-hours calls with another vet? Do they refer you to a veterinary emergency clinic? Know these answers before you have the emergency.

When you get some recommendations, and before you get your puppy, go visit each office. Things to keep in mind: Is the waiting area clean? Is there enough room for several animals without crowding? Do you like the office staff? Are their fees reasonable?

Even after you've chosen a veterinarian and made an appointment, if you decide you don't like that particular veterinarian, don't hesitate to try someone else. You and the vet will be working together for many years to keep your dog healthy, so you need to be able to talk to your veterinarian and to get answers. If a particular vet is unwilling to spend time explaining things to you, it may be time to find another doctor.

Other points to consider are acupuncture, chiropractic methods, homeopathic remedies and holistic treatments. Some veterinarians are strictly traditionalists; others incorporate other types of treatment into their practice. You need to be comfortable with these choices when you decide on your veterinarian.

*Ravyn Nicole is a bundle of holiday puppy joy.*

## ALTERNATIVE HEALING METHODS

In your search for an alternative veterinarian, you may see the initials TCM. TCM stands for Traditional Chinese Medicine, and that includes not only acupuncture but also herbal treatment. Many herbal compounds, when used correctly, may be gentler than synthetic compounds designed to produce the same result. Remember, though: just because herbs are "natural" doesn't mean that you can give them to your dog indiscriminately. Don't be tempted to diagnose and treat your dog yourself. Consult with a veterinarian who is trained to use herbs safely.

• **Acupuncture:** Acupuncturists use hair-fine needles to stimulate acupoints on the body. These points contain high levels of nerve endings and blood vessels. Acupuncture has been used for over 4,500 years on humans and for about 2,000 on animals. Acupuncture increases blood flow, which speeds healing and can also lower heart rate and improve the function of the immune system. An acupuncture treatment also encourages the release of endorphins, which are natural painkillers, as well as cortisal, an anti-inflammatory steroid.

Many veterinarians use acupuncture to complement Western medicine, making a diagnosis based on traditional medicine and then using the acupuncture to help ease pain and hasten healing. Acupuncture can help with such conditions as arthritis, allergies and skin conditions, as well as epilepsy and the side effects of cancer.

• **Chiropractic:** Chiropractic adjustments manipulate the spine and connecting bones on the theory that if the bones are out of alignment, this irritates the nerves and causes discomfort. A chiropractor gently pushes the bones back into alignment. Some people take their dogs to chiropractors for humans if they can't find a chiropractic veterinarian. If that's your choice, make sure that your veterinarian has examined your dog first to rule out other causes of soreness or lameness, such as a tumor.

• **Holistic treatments:** Holistic veterinarians consider the whole dog, not just individual parts. Rather than just treat symptoms, a holistic practitioner will consider the dog's physical and social environment in the diagnosis. A holistic vet is likely to use alternatives, such as acupuncture, chiropractic treatment and herbs as well as Western medicine.

• **Homeopathy:** Homeopathy is based on the theory that like heals like. A substance, frequently a plant, is diluted in stages so that it is harmless and free from side effects and then is used to treat various illnesses and symptoms. Homeopathic remedies come in liquid form, tablets, powders and ointments.

## CONSIDERING THE COSTS

The best things in life may be free, but their upkeep can be expensive. Having a puppy is certainly much cheaper than having a child. Your dog will never want the latest style in clothes (although you might want to dress him up in canine couture) or his own cell phone, and he won't ask for a car when he graduates from obedience school. Medical care is cheaper for dogs than it is for humans, but there are expenses. Depending on where you live and the size of your dog, spaying your dog can run upward of $150. The visit for an annual check-up and shots can be $100 or more. A six-month supply of heartworm preventative is around $40 for a medium-size dog, and $75–$100 buys you six months' worth of flea preventative. These are only estimates.

*Springer pup Misty snoozes with Santa.*

You may want to consider pet insurance to help with medical expenses. Some insurance plans cover only regular visits and offer nothing for major injuries or diseases. Some will cover certain conditions but may exclude certain breed-specific conditions or preexisting conditions. Know what you're getting before you start paying those monthly premiums.

## VACCINATION VISIT

Once you've chosen your veterinarian, it's time to make an appointment and take your puppy in for a visit. Depending on the age of your puppy, he will already have had one or two sets of vaccinations. Generally, shots are given to a puppy at 8, 12 and 16 weeks of

*"The weather outside is frightful!" thinks Jazzy.*

age, and then annually. When you bring your puppy home, your breeder should give you a record of shots already given; if not, ask for it. If you get your dog from a shelter, ask whether they have any vaccination or other medical records. Many animal shelters have the animals vaccinated before they go to new homes.

Vaccination protocol is changing rapidly. Veterinarians used to give vaccination boosters annually for just about everything there was a vaccination for. Combination shots typically contained vaccines for distemper, hepatitis, leptospirosis, parainfluenza and parvovirus, and then the rabies shot was also given at the

131

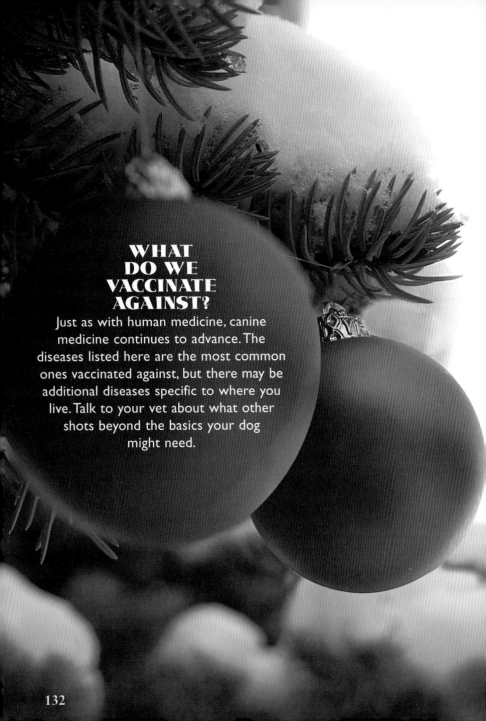

# WHAT DO WE VACCINATE AGAINST?

Just as with human medicine, canine medicine continues to advance. The diseases listed here are the most common ones vaccinated against, but there may be additional diseases specific to where you live. Talk to your vet about what other shots beyond the basics your dog might need.

**Rabies:** As mentioned, the rabies vaccination is required by law. Rabies is a fatal virus that attacks the central nervous system. It is spread through saliva, and common carriers are bats, foxes, raccoons and skunks. There is no cure for rabies.

**Distemper:** Distemper is a deadly, highly contagious virus with a very low recovery rate. Symptoms include coughing, vomiting and fever. Along with rabies, it's a "must have" shot.

**Parvovirus:** Puppies are particularly susceptible to this potentially fatal virus, which is highly contagious. Symptoms include vomiting, bloody diarrhea, fever, lethargy and depression.

**Leptospirosis:** Leptospirosis is caused by bacteria transmitted through the urine of rats and mice. The disease causes renal failure and can be fatal; however, unless your dog will be exposed to rats and mice, you may be able to skip this vaccine. Talk to your veterinarian about your options.

**Hepatitis:** This virus spreads through the feces and urine of dogs. Dogs can recover from mild and moderate cases in about a week, but severe cases can be fatal. If your dog has hepatitis, he may be reluctant to move, and his abdomen may be tender. In severe cases, he may vomit, cough and have diarrhea.

**Bordetella:** Bordetella, often called kennel cough, is a highly contagious airborne disease. Most boarding kennels require this vaccination before accepting your dog. The primary symptom is a dry, hacking cough. Kennel cough can be treated with antibiotics and is not usually serious.

**Lyme disease:** Lyme disease used to be a concern in only the eastern United States, but it is spreading. Deer ticks spread this disease, which results in lethargy, lameness and loss of appetite. Talk to your veterinarian about the threat of Lyme disease in your area.

same time. Now more vets are giving separate shots rather than combination shots and are scheduling separate appointments for some of the different vaccines. The reason for spreading out the shots is to help prevent adverse reactions.

When your puppy gets his shots, don't leave the vet's office right away. Stay for a while to see whether he reacts to the shots. A mild reaction may be just a bit of swelling at the site of the injection. A more severe reaction would be hives or swelling around the face. He could have diarrhea or vomit. If you have left the office and notice any of these symptoms, call your veterinarian.

*Glittery garland and a sparkly eyed Pomeranian pup.*

Another thing that is changing is the frequency of vaccinations. Many veterinarians are opting not to vaccinate every year. Ask your vet about this. Some vets still recommend annual shots for young dogs or dogs that travel a lot. For older stay-at-home dogs, every three years may be the recommendation. For most vaccinations, you and your vet can decide the frequency. The only exception is the rabies vaccination. This vaccination is required by law in every state. Some states specify an annual shot; others only require a booster every three years. Ask your vet about the law in your state.

## ICKY THINGS

Okay, that's not a phrase you're going to hear a lot during the holidays, but it's something you need to know about if you're going to keep your puppy healthy. The "icky things" we are talking about here are parasites, both internal and external.

Let's start with heartworms. Heartworms can kill your dog, and they are found in every state of the union. Mosquitoes transmit the larvae and, once in your dog's bloodstream, the larvae migrate to the heart, where they grow into large insidious worms that clog the heart and make it increasingly difficult for the heart to pump blood.

The good news is that there is a preventive. First, your vet will take a blood sample to make sure your dog doesn't already have heartworms. If the test is negative, he'll give you medicine to protect your pup. Most heartworm preventives are given once a month, and many protect against other parasites in addition to heartworms. Talk to your vet about which preventive is the best choice for your dog.

The other internal parasites most commonly found in dogs are usually various types of worms that find a cozy

*Ace is dressed in his North Pole best.*

home in your dog's intestines. Hookworms are bloodsuckers, and their multiple bites can cause blood to seep, which may give your dog dark tarry stools and either diarrhea or constipation. The loss of blood may mean pale mucous membranes on your dog, and he may cough or have a poor appetite. If you suspect worms, take a fecal sample to your vet for testing. If your dog has hookworms, your vet will prescribe the proper medicine for getting rid of the problem.

Whipworms are another nasty pest. These worms cause inflammation of the large bowel and may cause diarrhea, often with mucus and blood. Whipworm eggs can live in the soil for years, so if your dog is diagnosed with whipworms, you'll need to test on a regular basis to catch any recurrence of the worm. Paving over the soil is the only way to get rid of the worm eggs in the soil.

Ascarid roundworms are common in puppies, so most puppies are automatically given a dewormer for roundworms. If your puppy has a round, distended abdomen, a poor appetite or soft stools, he may have roundworms. Adults can also get roundworms, and the symptoms are the same, but the worms are not as harmful to adults as they are to puppies.

Tapeworms are the least harmful of all of the worms your dog can get, but they should not be ignored, as they rob your dog of nutrients. Tapeworm segments look like tiny grains of rice in your dog's stool. Your dog can get tapeworms from eating a flea as well as from eating a bird or a small mammal. If you suspect tapeworms, talk to your vet. It usually takes only one dose of deworming medication to eradicate the tapeworms.

External parasites are creepy crawlies that can irritate your pet and spread disease. The most common

*Ten-month-old Dutch Shepherd mix Bella is ready to help pull the sleigh.*

*Lucy's just hanging around, waiting
for the festivities to begin.*

external parasites are fleas and ticks, and both suck your dog's blood. Mosquitoes are also bloodsuckers and, while not as likely to be as big a problem, can spread both heartworm and West Nile virus.

One flea can bite a dog as many as 400 times in one day. Ouch! Imagine how many bites that would be if your dog had a large infestation of the nasty critters. Besides the threat of anemia, your dog may be allergic to flea saliva and will bite and chew at himself because the saliva makes him itch. All of the dog's biting and chewing can result in nasty sores that are much worse than the original flea bite(s).

To check for fleas, roll your puppy over and check his tummy, especially near the hind legs, where the hair is thinner. You may see a flea or two scurrying for cover or you may not see a flea but may notice little black flecks. These flecks may be "flea dirt" (flea feces). To tell whether this is regular dirt or flea dirt, gather a few of the flecks, put them on a paper towel and dampen the towel. If the black flecks turn red, it's flea dirt—and time to declare war!

The best thing to do is to stop the problem before it starts by using a flea preventive from your vet. There are several products on the market, and some fight ticks and mosquitoes as well as fleas. Talk to your vet about what's best for your puppy.

If you find that your puppy or dog has become infested, give him a bath and wash his bedding. You will also have to vacuum all carpets and furniture and wash blankets, pillows and throw rugs. Regular vacuuming will help control fleas in the house. Cut up a flea collar and put it in the bag or canister of your vacuum, and remember to empty the vacuum cleaner (or change bags) frequently so it doesn't turn into a condo for fleas.

# HOW TO GIVE MEDICINE

It's inevitable that during your dog's lifetime you will need to give medicines now and then. Pills are probably the easiest form of medicine to give to a dog. If your dog will do anything for food, just hide the pill in a bit of cream cheese or peanut butter. If you are giving the pills at mealtime, hide the pill in a spoonful of canned food. Yogurt that contains active cultures is another good choice. Dogs like it, and it helps put good bacteria back into the digestive system that an antibiotic may kill. My own male is such a chow hound that I can drop most pills into his dry food, and he'll gobble it down.

Some dogs, however, are more discerning than others. Some will eat the good stuff from around the pill and leave just the pill in the bottom of the bowl. With a dog like that, try crushing the pill and mixing the powder into yogurt or vanilla ice cream. If your dog still sticks up his nose, you'll have to give the pill yourself. Straddle your dog to help hold him in place, then tilt his muzzle up, place one hand over the top of his muzzle, and squeeze his top lip against his teeth. This should make him open his mouth. Throw the pill to the back of his mouth, close his jaws, and, still pointing his muzzle up, gently stroke his throat until he swallows.

Liquids can be a bit trickier, unless they taste good. If the medicine has a flavor that your dog likes, just squirt the liquid over his food. Using canned food is still a good idea, as it might just roll off the kibble. If you have to "do it yourself," once again straddle your dog. Pull his lower lip out to make a pocket, pour the liquid into the pocket, and then let the lip go and gently hold your dog's muzzle closed until he swallows.

A flea infestation can take a while to get rid of. Even if the fleas are no longer on your pet and your dog has been treated with a preventative, the fleas can still live in the environment in their different life stages. Ask your vet to recommend a safe flea treatment that you can use on your carpets and furniture.

Ticks may or may not be a problem where you live. You're more likely to find ticks in tall grass, shrubs or wooded areas than in short grass or paved areas. Besides making like vampires and sucking your puppy's blood, ticks can transmit diseases, such as Rocky Mountain spotted fever, Lyme disease and tick paralysis.

*Samantha Claus is spreading holiday cheer.*

You may not see a tick if it's hidden in your dog's hair, but you might feel it. If you live where ticks are a threat, push your dog's hair aside and check his skin. If you find a tick, use tweezers to remove it. Grasp the tick firmly and pull gently and slowly. Don't crush or squeeze the tick, or you may leave its head behind in your dog.

Don't touch the tick; if you do, wash your hands immediately. Flush the tick down the toilet or drop it into a container of alcohol. Wash the area where the tick was on your dog. If you can't remove the tick yourself or are afraid to try, take your dog to the vet's office. Never leave ticks on your dog.

Here's another "never": never use a cigarette or any type of flame to remove a tick. There's no doubt that fire will get the tick's attention, but you could also burn your dog.

## SPAYING AND NEUTERING

If you're not going to show or breed your puppy, it's a good idea to spay or neuter. Ideally, you should do this before your dog reaches sexual maturity. With males, this usually happens sometime between the ages of 6 and 18 months. Your male puppy will start to lift his leg when he urinates. He'll start marking his territory, letting other dogs know that your yard is his turf. Your walks will become less walking and more bush sniffing and leg lifting. Your male may become less tolerant of other males. He will definitely take an interest in girls. When a male dog smells a female in season, he has one thought only: find her! If he gets loose, he will follow the seductive scent wherever it leads, and obeying you if you call him will be far down on his to-do list. A male may also decide to mark his indoor territory, choosing table legs and couches. Neutering before this behavior starts will prevent it from ever

### SENIOR CARE

Dogs are typically considered seniors at around seven years of age, and many vets recommend twice-yearly check-ups for senior dogs. Catching a problem early on is important at any age, but especially so for older dogs.

*"Waiting for Santa is exhausting," thinks
Basset Hound Hunk Heartbreaker.*

occurring. Neutering can also prevent prostate problems and cancer in males.

Females will also reach maturity sometime between the ages of 6 and 18 months. This is marked by the female's coming into "season" or "heat." Females come into heat about every six months, and this is marked by a bloody discharge. A heat cycle lasts 21 days, but she is receptive to a male for only 3 to 5 of those days. If you have both a male and a female, you will have to keep the two of them separated while she's in heat. A male in love can be pretty persistent, as well as vocal, and three weeks of whining and crying can be a long time.

If you have a fenced yard, make sure that there are no holes or gaps in the fence and that the fence is high enough to keep out any wandering neighborhood males. When

*Mya is ready for Christmas... with bells on!*

walking your girl, keep a firm grip on the lead and keep a sharp lookout for any amorous males.

Spaying your female will eliminate these heat cycles, with some added health benefits. Spaying before she comes into season can help reduce the possibility of mammary tumors. Removing the uterus also eliminates the possibility of your female getting uterine cancer or pyometra, the latter of which is an infection of the uterus.

## COMMON HEALTH PROBLEMS

Dogs are generally a pretty healthy species, but there are problems that may be size or breed specific. For instance, hip dysplasia can occur in any dog, but the larger the dog, the more prone to this problem he will be. Hip dysplasia is a disease that affects the head of the femur, where it fits into the socket of the hip joint. The round head of the femur becomes misshapen and no longer fits snugly into the joint. In severe cases, it may pop out altogether. Hip replacement surgery is possible, depending on how severe the case, and there are medications and therapeutic options to help with lameness and pain. If you're getting a dog to be a jogging partner or to compete in agility, ask the breeder about the possibility of hip dysplasia. A good breeder will breed only from dogs that have certified healthy hips, thus lessening the risk of hip dysplasia in the offspring.

In toy breeds, patellar luxation is frequently a problem. This translates as a kneecap that pops out of its groove. When the kneecap, or patella, is dislocated, the dog will limp and be in pain. Sometimes the kneecap pops back into place on its own; sometimes it requires a veterinarian's help.

Von Willebrand's disease is a blood-clotting disorder, similar to hemophilia in people. It can occur in any breed, but many herding breeds seem to be particularly susceptible.

*Bailey (left) and Winston (right) were
thrilled to be chosen as the two newest reindeer.*

*Browning is the cutest Christmas chocolate ever.*

Mange is a skin problem to watch for. There are two types of mange, both caused by tiny mites. With sarcoptic mange, there is intense itching and, with advanced cases, skin lesions and hair loss. A dog may receive medication, or a topical treatment, or a combination of both. The course of treatment usually lasts for three weeks. The dog's bedding should be either thoroughly disinfected or thrown away and replaced. This type of mange is transmittable to other animals and humans.

Demodectic mange is passed from the mother to the puppies and affects puppies between the ages of three and ten months. With demodectic mange, you may notice hair loss around the eyes or lips or on the forelegs. The dog may also lose hair at the tips of the ears. Demodectic mange doesn't cause the itching that sarcoptic mange does, and it is usually diagnosed from skin scrapings. A special shampoo may be prescribed along with medication. It is sometimes recommended that the dog's coat be clipped down to maximize the effectiveness of the shampoo. Demodectic mange, if not widespread on the dog's body, may go away on its own. If it spreads beyond small localized areas, it may need up to a year of treatment. It is not contagious.

## FIRST AID

I have had dogs for over 30 years, and outside of cleaning out a few wounds and stopping a bit of bleeding now and then, I've never needed to practice much in the way of first aid. That doesn't mean I don't have a few basic supplies handy "just in case," and it doesn't mean I don't think about first aid techniques. I do. I learned years ago that the first thing to do in an emergency is to take a deep breath. That breath can help you think, and knowing a bit about first aid can help you to act calmly and recognize just how serious a problem might be.

*Puppy Destiny is tearing right into Christmas!*

# Puppy's First Christmas

*Rum-pa-pa-pum!*

To start, consider taking a course in canine first aid. Call your local Red Cross chapter or check with the local animal shelter or dog-training school to see whether they offer such a class. Alternatively, you might invest in a basic first aid book for dogs or talk to your veterinarian about what he suggests for emergency situations.

It's important to know how to take your dog's temperature. You'll need a rectal thermometer, and you'll need to know that a dog's normal temperature is

*Ava Lil' Love has love to give all year 'round.*

between 100 and 102.5 degrees F. If the temperature is below 100 or above 103, call your vet.

Have your veterinarian show you how to take your dog's pulse. The easiest way is to find the femoral artery, high on a hind leg, almost into the groin area. A dog's pulse rate will be between 80 and 140. The smaller the dog, the higher the pulse rate will be.

Since many first aid items are the same for both people and dogs, you don't necessarily need a separate kit. You don't even need a kit, as such, but you should keep all your first aid supplies on the same shelf or in the same cupboard to save time in an emergency. If you

*J.D. (left) and Riley (right)*
*are ready to party!*

choose to put together a kit, a small fishing tackle box works well, or you can buy a doggie first aid kit from a pet-supply store or vendor.

Basics include 3% hydrogen peroxide for cleaning wounds and for inducing vomiting, a roll of gauze, gauze pads, adhesive tape, small scissors, tweezers, thermometer, children's Benadryl for allergic reactions to insect stings (give one milligram per pound of your dog's weight), children's aspirin (give one tablet per 10–15 pounds of body weight), liquid tears, antibiotic salve and vet wrap. Vet wrap will hold gauze or splints in place but won't stick to your dog's fur. Pet-supply sources sell it, or maybe you can get a roll or two from your vet.

Other useful products to have on hand are Pepto-Bismol, Kaopectate and aloe vera. Pepto-Bismol can help control vomiting and diarrhea. Give one teaspoon per 20 pounds of weight every 4 hours. For diarrhea, give one teaspoon per five pounds of dog every one to three hours. Aloe vera can relieve many skin irritations, including bug bites and hot spots. Besides being safe, it is also bitter, so it may discourage licking, which can slow healing time. You may safely give your dog aspirin, but ask your vet before giving either acetaminophen or ibuprofen, as these can be harmful to your dog.

For those of you who prefer to use natural products as much as possible, cayenne pepper can help stop bleeding when applied to a wound, calendula gel and comfrey ointment can be applied topically to help healing, and arnica gel can be applied to sprains, strains and bruises.

If your dog gets hurt badly, you may need to muzzle him. Even the gentlest dog can snap or bite when in pain. If you have a muzzle in your first aid kit,

# SKUNKS AND PORCUPINES

If you live in an area with porcupines, your dog may some day meet one and, trust me, if there's an argument, your dog will get the worst of it. You can, if you are very brave, remove quills with a pair of pliers, but it's not the best idea in the world. Porcupine quills have barbs at the end that make pulling them out painful. Assuming you, or you and a helper or two, could hold your dog, he would be in pain and he could bite. You could also miss a quill or two, and those overlooked quills would work further into the body. Even a vet can miss a quill.

Years ago, our first dog tangled with a porcupine. We took her to the vet, but a month later, when we returned because she was limping, X-rays showed a quill that had worked its way to the bone, and our dog required surgery. The best course of action is to take your dog to the vet to be anesthetized and have the quills removed.

The traditional treatment for a dog that's been perfumed by a skunk used to be tomato juice; that's not only messy but also ineffective. You end up with a smelly pink dog. If you have nothing better on hand, plain vinegar will do a better job, although it's not perfect. The best remedy seems to be a solution of one quart hydrogen peroxide, 1/4 cup baking soda and one teaspoon of liquid dish soap. You need to mix it and use it quickly, as it loses power after about an hour, and you can't premix it, as it will explode if it's in a covered container.

Be very careful not to get the mixture in your dog's eyes. Work the mixture into the coat and let it sit a few minutes. You may need to rinse and repeat.

fine. Otherwise, use a length of gauze for a muzzle. Stand behind your dog and loop the gauze under his muzzle. Tie a half-knot on top of the muzzle, then take the ends back under the muzzle and tie another half-knot. Bring the ends of gauze up behind the ears and tie an easy-to-release knot or bow. Make your ties firm, but not too tight.

If you have a dog like a Pug or a Shih Tzu or any other breed with a short nose, a muzzle may not be practical. You don't want to restrict breathing in any way; you just want to avoid getting bitten. So wrap a magazine around your dog's head so that the ends extend out past his nose. Or wrap him in a blanket with the ends extending out past the head. This will keep your dog from turning his head and will help keep his muzzle away from you while you work.

If you suspect that your dog has ingested something poisonous, call the Pet Poison Helpline at (800) 213-6680 or the ASPCA Animal Poison Control Center at (888) 426-4435. Both of these services charge a fee. If you know what your dog swallowed and it's organic, you can administer 3% hydrogen peroxide (1 or 2 teaspoons about every 10–15 minutes until he vomits), but never encourage vomiting if a dog has swallowed something caustic. Instead, give him lots of milk or vegetable oil to help coat his digestive tract.

Before dashing off to your veterinarian's, take the time to call first. This gives the staff time to prepare for the emergency, which will save time when your dog arrives. If you are transporting a dog with spinal injuries, carry him on a blanket or board and try to move him as little as possible.

With luck, you and your dog will never face a medical emergency, but it doesn't hurt to follow the Boy Scouts' motto and be prepared.

It's the New Year, and the party's over, but the fun's just beginning. Unlike Christmas goodies that were eaten long ago, unlike presents that didn't really fit or are already broken, you've got a new family member who will be with you for many years and will always be ready for a game of fetch or a cuddle on the sofa.

Of course, responsibilities come along with all that fun. Your puppy will still need frequent trips outdoors, so now's the time to consider the daily schedule. With school and work back in session, you may have to put more thought into who's watching the puppy. If someone works at home or is home most of the time, then the situation is ideal, but even with everyone gone, you should be able to put together a schedule that will continue the puppy's house-training.

In the mornings, you may have to get up a bit earlier to accommodate feeding, walking and playing with the puppy. Then, put your puppy in his crate or pen. Over the years, I've been lucky enough to have jobs that enabled me to leave at noon to get home and take care of dogs, but not everyone has that luxury. If no one in the family can get home at noon, see whether there's a friend

*It's Christmas puppy Kringle . . .
what an appropriate name!*

or relative who's willing to stop by and let the puppy out. Maybe there's a neighbor who'd enjoy playing with the puppy or who would agree to help out in return for an invitation to dinner or a batch of homemade cookies. If none of these choices is an option, consider contacting a pet sitter for that noon break.

Doggie day care may be another choice once your puppy has had all of his shots. Besides having someone look after him, day care will give your pup a chance to play with other dogs and get some exercise when no one is at home.

If someone does take care of your puppy at noon, then the puppy can easily wait to go out again until a child arrives home from school. If you don't have children, then you may need a dog walker again in the afternoon unless you can make arrangements to get home early for the afternoon walk.

Your evening schedule should be a lot like what it was over the holidays. Remember

## LESS STRESS

Give yourself extra time in the morning so that you can go through your normal routine and leave the house in a calm manner. You don't want to create a stressful atmosphere that will make the pup anxious about being home alone.

*Eight-week-old Maltese Spunky Spice is
sparkling with holiday cheer.*

*Puppy Snyder Lou takes a break from the holiday hustle and bustle.*

that even if you're tired from your day at work or school, your puppy still needs attention and playtime. It's easy to play fetch and watch television at the same time; just remember to use a soft toy or ball to reduce the risk of damage in the house.

With the holidays over and a long winter stretching ahead, now's the time to consider school for your puppy. See whether anyone in your area offers puppy kindergarten classes or beginning obedience or rally classes. Many boarding kennels will bring in a trainer for classes, or maybe your local YMCA has classes. In my area, the humane society offers clicker classes.

Once your dog is mature, you might want to explore agility or teach your dog to track. Conformation showing (like the dog shows on TV) is for pure-breds, but mixed breeds are allowed to compete in sports like obedience, agility, flyball and more. Training for and participating in these activities are great ways to bond with your dog and for both of you to get some exercise.

Your puppy will be a puppy for only a little while, and there will never be another "puppy's first Christmas," but there will be many more Christmases to share with your new best friend, and that's a gift you won't want to exchange.

## DO YOUR RESEARCH

If you plan to use a doggie day care or dog walker, do your research in advance. Visit local day care facilities or look for dog walkers who are insured; you can interview them and have them meet your puppy. You want to be comfortable with your pup's caretaker.

*Tucker is a handsome addition to the Christmas décor.*

# Index